# ROUTLEDGE LIBRARY EDITIONS: SOVIET SOCIETY

Volume 22

# SOVIET RUSSIA FIGHTS NEUROSIS

# SOVIET RUSSIA FIGHTS NEUROSIS

## FRANKWOOD E. WILLIAMS

Routledge
Taylor & Francis Group

LONDON AND NEW YORK

First published in 1934 by George Routledge & Sons, Ltd.

This edition first published in 2025
by Routledge
4 Park Square, Milton Park, Abingdon, Oxon OX14 4RN

and by Routledge
605 Third Avenue, New York, NY 10158

*Routledge is an imprint of the Taylor & Francis Group, an informa business*

© 1934

*British Library Cataloguing in Publication Data*
A catalogue record for this book is available from the British Library

ISBN: 978-1-032-86028-2 (Set)
ISBN: 978-1-032-86474-7 (Volume 22) (hbk)
ISBN: 978-1-032-86476-1 (Volume 22) (pbk)
ISBN: 978-1-003-52770-1 (Volume 22) (ebk)

DOI: 10.4324/9781003527701

**Publisher's Note**
The publisher has gone to great lengths to ensure the quality of this reprint but points out that some imperfections in the original copies may be apparent.

**Disclaimer**
The publisher has made every effort to trace copyright holders and would welcome correspondence from those they have been unable to trace.

# SOVIET RUSSIA
# FIGHTS NEUROSIS

By
FRANKWOOD E. WILLIAMS
M.D.

LONDON
GEORGE ROUTLEDGE & SONS, LTD.
BROADWAY HOUSE: 68-74 CARTER LANE, E.C.
1934

Printed in Great Britain by Butler & Tanner Ltd., Frome and London

*To*
MARY ROSS
AND
ARTHUR KELLOGG

# CONTENTS

# PREFACE

So much is written and spoken about Russia that one becomes confused. What is one to believe? For every favourable statement, one can find from an apparently equally authoritative person, an unfavourable statement. Not only is the Russian experiment as a whole differently described, explained or evaluated, but the same street incident or item in the larger plan is reported favourably by one observer and unfavourably by another. Even though we disregard obvious prejudice in either direction, we are still left confused by the differences between those who, it would seem, are endeavouring to observe and to report fairly and objectively. At least two reasons for these differences, however, are easily discernible.

A manufacturer who has built up an efficient organization that now turns out a maximum of product with a minimum of lost effort visits a tractor plant in Russia. The fact that he has come to Russia at all might indicate that he is a somewhat liberal and socially minded individual who is not altogether satisfied with social conditions as they are, who believes there should be some changes, and who is curious to see what changes the Russians have really made and how things actually " work ". His standard is efficiency. He is an expert and his training and experience have fitted him to recognize and appreciate skilled workmanship.

Ready, perhaps even eager to be favourably impressed,

he enters the tractor factory. He is shown through every department; everything is laid out before him. Officials discuss with him frankly their successes and their failures. He listens to what he is told, observes with his own eyes, and before an hour is over is shocked at what he has found. Such inefficiency he has never seen! From this nothing can come! Scarcely the first principles of efficiency and skill have been learned, he thinks. And when he learns that in this factory a large percentage of the finished product is defective and must be scrapped he throws up his hands. Unheard of! Outrageous! Ruinous! Not in fifty years, if ever, will the Russians be able to manufacture efficiently! If this is an example of the efficiency of Russian production then the Russian plan is doomed to failure. He returns home, reports accurately what he has seen and heard, and with the honest judgment just given.

Another person visits the same tractor plant, observes the same things, hears the same reports from officials. To him, however, the extraordinary thing is not that a large percentage of the finished produce is defective but that a still larger percentage of it is actually good. When he recalls that most of the thousands of workers in this plant, now engaged upon the most skilled of operations, five years ago were peasants on the land who could neither read nor write, who did not know what any ten-year-old schoolboy knows about machines, who never had seen a modern machine, perhaps not even an iron wheel—when he recalls that it is these people, not a group of skilled industrial workers, who in this comparatively short time have sufficiently mastered the intricacies of machine manufacture as to be able to turn out a product more than fifty per cent successfully, he believes that this is one of the amazing things of history. And when he considers what this has all meant in terms of personal development of these thousands of workers, and of what their work means, even if only in part efficient, to the lives of thousands upon thousands of others, his amazement at the ramification and significance of all this grows. *He* returns, reports precisely what he saw and heard, and fairly stutters in his effort to tell others what to him it seems to mean.

Another visits Russia and here and there sees long queues of men, women and children waiting before stores, perhaps in the sun, perhaps in a drizzly rain, for oil or food. He goes slowly by the queue observing the signs of weariness, of unhappiness, of misery, perhaps even " agony " in the faces and bodies of these people. He returns and describes what he saw. Another passes the same queue and observes also. In the faces of the people, however, he finds no great fatigue, no misery, no pain, but a patient waiting as though there were all the time in the world and no hurry, even satisfaction, for at the end of the queue there is what they have come for and it will be obtained as the turn comes, whereas for many years there has been waiting in queues both hot and dusty, wet and freezing only to find nothing at the end.

It is probably impossible for any of us to be completely objective. The report of the second observer may not be wholly objective, but the report of the first may arouse our suspicion—usually confirmed by the fact that gloom, misery, and suffering is reported in almost everything observed—that unconsciously the observer has utilized a mental mechanism well known to psychiatrists, and to others also, for that matter, although not under a technical name, that of identifying oneself with the thing observed and then believing that the observed feels as the observer would feel in the same situation. The observer is not aware that this is what he is doing. He does not know that he is not reporting how the people feel who are standing in that queue, as shown by the expressions on their faces, but merely how he would feel if he had to stand in that queue for an hour in order to get a can of oil. Not knowing that this is what he is doing, his report and opinion must be considered honest, although it is an honesty that cannot count for much.

These two examples at least indicate why there can be such diverse reports and opinions from honest and sincere people returning from Russia, many of them experts in their particular field. The manufacturer, using a measure with which he was thoroughly familiar, found truly a serious deficiency, but allowed himself to be blinded to other equally important aspects by the very tool he brought with him. The first observer of the food queue fell into a psychological trap that he has often, indeed, fallen into at home without knowing it, but which had its best opportunity for use in the totally new environment of Russia.

Now it is perfectly possible, of course, for the same psychological mechanism to work in an opposite direction, for people of integrity to judge and report all too favourably. Surprisingly enough, perhaps, but for a very obvious reason, this is less likely to happen. An individual here who, for reasons of personal need, perhaps of inadequacy and frustration and inability to compete in a highly competitive society, builds up within himself a hot enthusiasm for Russia, builds up a dream world that does not exist. On visiting Russia, therefore, the reality is so far from his dream that instead of bringing back glowing and exaggerated reports he is likely to bring back very tepid reports, or reports bitter with his disillusionment.

As between these various reports, then, how are we to know what is true ? There is no sure way. It would be helpful, however, if we could know more about those who write and speak on Russia. But what we need most to know it is impossible to know, which is something in regard to the emotional " set ", or " pattern ", of the individual, what his usual day-to-day reactions are to various types of situations. If I know, for example, that a person invariably reacts against anything new, then I have a clue to his description of Russia. If, on the other hand, I know that to anything new a person invariably reacts favourably, then I have another clue. But there are many subtle ways of reacting between these two extremes, and many more things to react to than just " newness ". These things we cannot know except as we have personal acquaintance with the individual.

The most we can know, perhaps, is something in regard to the background, general experience and training of the individual, although we must not put too great emphasis upon professional training, for, while such training is important in the limited field of the training, it is not a certificate of an individual's ability to evaluate human situations outside his own technical field. For professional training is but an outer coating, no matter how high the polish, laid over the *original man* trained. To a technical problem within his field a trained person will react with his training. To more general human situations outside his field the *original man* will react and that person may be no more, even less, trustworthy than the humblest person about. However, all such information is helpful.

For whatever help it may be, therefore, in determining the possible accuracy or inaccuracy of what I have written here in regard to Russia, let me say this in regard to myself:

I am a physician. In the field of medicine my speciality is psychiatry. For the past twenty years, as physician and psychiatrist, I have been working in the field of human relations, which means the relationship of one individual to another, of the individual to the group, and of the group to the individual. The problems one deals with have to do with marital, home, or domestic relationships, juvenile and adult delinquency, nervous and mental illness, the maladjusted child in the school or the home, the child-teacher and parent-child relationship, the emotional development of children and the special problems of adolescence. Broadly, this is called " mental hygiene ".

I have never been a " radical ". In social matters I have been just an ordinary citizen, interested mostly in my own work and so far as political and social matters were concerned, inclined towards some sort of " liberalism ". Extremist radicals I have always looked upon as rather wild, " half-crazy ", neurotic or at least seriously maladjusted people who probably should not, indeed, be sent by magistrates to jail but rather to a psychiatric clinic where the psychiatrists might be able to do something for them. Before my first visit to Russia I knew about as much regarding Communism and Karl Marx and the social experiment in Russia as the average citizen, which I take to be not much, and was about that much interested. My first visit to Russia was a more or less casual one as a part of a summer holiday in Europe. Being in Berlin I just dropped over, as it were, to Moscow and Leningrad to have a look round to see what these strange people might be doing in my own field. That there might be something to see I had gathered from the remarks of Dr. L. Rosenstein, one of the Russian delegates to The First International Congress on Mental Hygiene held in Washington, D.C., in May 1930. I received such a shock on this first visit that there was nothing to do but to go back the next year to prove to myself, at least, that what I thought I had seen on my first brief visit was actually true. This led to a journey of over ten thousand miles from one end of European Russia to the other, through cities, towns and villages, factories, hospitals, schools, prisons, wherever I could poke my nose—and I found I could poke it anywhere I wanted to. If I came away from my first visit shocked and stirred, I came away from my second visit deeply thoughtful.

One does not make up one's mind all at once about the experiment in Russia. One is too shaken and there is too much to think about. At least, so I have found it. Gradually one's thoughts begin to take form. From time to time during the past two years, as my thoughts on any particular matter have seemed to become clear I have written them out, more for myself as a means of further clearing my own mind than for anyone else. What the various chapters of this book really represent are my own effort to think out for myself the problems raised by my former professional and life experiences, and myself as a person, coming in contact with an entirely different professional and life experience and person as found in Russia.  To some who have read what I have written, this thinking out on my part has seemed to be helpful in clearing up some of their own thinking.  It is their judgment I take in putting these papers into book form, and, in doing so, roughly in the order in which I have thought them out.  If in the end I seem more sure than in the beginning, it is because in two years some things seem clearer to me.

In a sense, perhaps, these papers should not be published at all for the very reason that they are just the fumbling along, the thinking out loud, with no audience whatsoever in mind—the thinking one must do to have any peace at all with oneself, of one whose knowledge and experience had been challenged and who was seeking a resolution of the conflict thus aroused.  They may, therefore, be too personal and individual to have value for others.  But, after all, what are any of us doing but struggling along trying to find our way, and what more can we do than to exchange honestly our thoughts and experiences, to say to another as clearly as we can what really we do think knowing full well that we may be wrong but that we have been as right as we could be?  It is in this spirit that this book is presented.  It need disturb no one too much.  If anything I have said is true then that is the important thing and must be reckoned with, not my statement of it; if anything I have said is not true, then printing it in a book does not make it true and no great harm can come of it.  That some may be deceived and believe it true is not very important, for they will soon be undeceived and will have learned something that it is important for them to know in the process.

I should call attention particularly to one possible misunderstanding, however. I have frequently used such expressions as " the psychiatrist thinks ", or " according to the psychiatric point of view ", and the like. It should be understood that when one uses such expressions it is largely as a matter of convenience. No one psychiatrist can speak for all other psychiatrists any more than one lawyer, clergyman or mathematician can speak for all others in his profession. In each profession there is indeed a central core of knowledge about which there is little or no dispute, but as one proceeds from the centre out towards the periphery of the professional field these agreements become less frequent. This is particularly so in psychiatry, where training and experience differ widely, and very particularly so when matters fall without the range of classifiable mental disease, the range of most psychiatric training, and enter upon the field of personality and social problems. Here one finds agreement with a smaller group or may not find agreement at all. While in many instances, perhaps in most, I feel there would be general agreement as to my view among psychiatrists, it is better for the reader to assume that I speak for myself rather than for psychiatrists in general.[1]

[1] As this matter of " disagreement among ' experts ' " gives difficulty to so many people, it might be well to press the matter a little further. That in making observations there should be, in any given instance, differences of opinion as to what has been observed is understandable ; the observed fact having been agreed upon, it is understandable also that there should be differences of opinion in interpreting these facts. We are not concerned with this which would seem quite simple and common to all professions, although it is often confusing even to members of other professions—when it occurs in another profession.

What concerns us is this : medical training, as no doubt

Rabbi Lazaron has permitted me to include his article, " Confusion Less Confounded : A Rabbi Takes Up the Challenge of a Psychiatrist ", in reply to Chapter V : " Out From Confusion ".  Indeed he has done me the courtesy of granting this permission before it was possible for me to furnish him with a copy of my reply, " Hate : Confusion Worse Confounded ".  I wished to include this paper, for I know no abler statement of the

training in other professions, does not cover the entire field as found in practice.  The physician, for example, has not received in his medical training instruction, which means to be presented with objectively obtained and considered data, concerning problems that formerly were, and, in large part, still are, considered " moral " problems.  Problems of sexual hygiene, the frequency and mode of intercourse, masturbation, and the like, are examples of this.  As these problems come in the mind of the community to be associated with hygiene rather than with morals, however, they are brought more and more frequently to the physician rather than to the priest. But the physician has no special knowledge from his training and, unless his professional experience has led him to a study of the particular problem, his advice, given as medical advice, is based only upon his own " moral " view or his own personal experience.  A thing is, therefore, " good " if it has been good for him and " bad " if it has been bad for him ; it is " moral " if he has no feeling about the matter, or if, perhaps, for purely personal reasons, he finds himself in rebellion against an opposite earlier moral training ; or it is " immoral " if it is not in harmony with what he was taught as a child and if no emotional reason exists for him to be in rebellion against this.

The same situation is to be found in the field of psychiatry where training has not concerned itself with many problems which were not formerly considered psychiatric but " moral " or " social " and where further professional experience, either through lack of opportunity or indisposition, has not led to a study of these problems.  Here the psychiatrist, when consulted, must likewise fall back upon early moral, religious and social training, and although his advice is given as " psychiatric ", and that implies scientific, it has no more scientific foundation than the advice of any other person who early received the position of modern religion, and the quality of the paper is only to be obtained by reading it as a whole. To attempt to summarize it, paraphrase it or to quote here and there from it would be to do it a serious injustice. I wish also to express my indebtedness to Dr. L. Rosenstein, Director of the Institute for Neuro-Psychiatric Prophylaxis in Moscow for his graciousness and assistance at all times.

### FRANKWOOD E. WILLIAMS.

same moral, religious and social training. That this makes for a wide difference of opinion can be easily understood. That there is, after all, a difference in value between the opinion of a psychiatrist, or general physician, and the opinion of another equally intelligent person for the reason that the psychiatrist at least brings to the consideration of a problem new to him a " trained " mind, does not help matters ; indeed, it tends to make it more difficult. A " trained " mind, working not on the basis of objective, impersonal knowledge, but upon the basis of subjective, personal experience, can be very dangerous. It has prestige in the first place, and therefore inspires confidence, and, in the second place, it appears to do one thing while doing another and can (here is where the training is applied) make what it is doing and its opinion seem reasonable and right.

# SOVIET RUSSIA FIGHTS NEUROSIS

## CHAPTER I

### THOSE CRAZY RUSSIANS

I WENT to Russia to study mental hygiene. I had been led to believe that things were being accomplished there that are impossible here. What I found was that the difference was the difference between our philosophies of life. In America, as in Britain, we live in a democracy with supposedly equal opportunity for all and personal progress dependent upon the success of our competition with others. In Russia under Communism—but what I found in Russia did not come easily; it meant recasting my whole approach to what I had been looking for. Let me first point out, then, as a stepping-stone, that concerning individual vicissitudes under democracy, it has been our view, based on what we thought we knew of personal mental hygiene, that outward circumstance does not produce the devastating mental effect that it is commonly supposed to do. It may be the straw that breaks the camel's back but it is not the cause of the weakness in the camel's back.

A business man develops insomnia because of worry over his business. The insomnia is not primarily due to difficulties in the business, but the state of the business may be the factor that will tip his insecurity balance far enough to produce the insomnia; or it may be the situation he will grasp to explain or excuse an insomnia not otherwise explicable to him. What are the problems involved? The insomnia is not a *mental-hygiene* problem—he is already ill. The mental-hygiene problem is, how to arrange matters so that neither he nor anyone else will need to have insomnia. There are two approaches to this: so arrange business that a condition cannot arise to cause him enough anxiety to upset his psychological balance (absurd); or, looking to the future, so direct his emotional development that a crisis will be unable to upset his balance (probably also absurd).

We recognize in America that there are, so far as we can see, only these two ways out and yet each seems quite impossible. It would be an optimist who would believe that business could ever be anything but " the race to the swift, the devil take the hindmost " and this must induce almost continuous anxiety. There is therefore no fundamental mental-hygiene effort in this direction here. Our attack is more along the lines of child training and development—but without much conviction of important success, unless over a very long time, because it must be done in an atmosphere of competition and rivalry that vitiates everything from the start and at every step. Further, whatever we may do in this direction, our work as mental hygienists has little relationship to anything else. It is but an incident among many other unrelated things. There is co-operative effort, to be sure, but each unit in the co-operation is a unit, after all, with its own responsibilities and aims and the joint enterprise is but incidental in any instance. There is no focus, only foci. There is no unity of activity; there is no one goal that we all have definitely in mind.

Russia, without apparently being aware of the impossibility, has grappled with both these absurdities; directly with the first, only indirectly with the second. (And when I speak of " Russia " I mean new Russia, not old Russia or the mixture of what is left of old and new; and not of something altogether accomplished but of something very definitely in the making.) The first is attacked by a sweeping effort to relieve anxiety pressures—precisely those pressures which in our society accumulate until the balance is upset and the strongest individual finds himself in difficulty—if it is no more (and it is quite enough) than with a middle-aged discouragement, bitterness, cynicism, frustration; or anxiety in regard to work, food, housing, personal progress, vocational and professional opportunity, sex life, marriage and the establishment of a family, illness, education of children, future security of a family.

In so far as this social relief of anxiety is successful it leaves the individual at the level of his anxiety-potential as he entered life at adolescence. What can that mean ? No one can tell. One can easily believe that it may mean a great deal. Certainly in a population of 160 millions it must be a parole for hundreds of thousands. That it can be enough one cannot grant, regardless of the optimism of the Russians, unless we are entirely wrong in regard to the ætiology of anxiety. But if we are right in regard to the ætiology of anxiety, then the Russians are right in their approach to the problem as a whole, for the fundamental ætiology can be attacked only indirectly and only as an accompaniment of tremendous social change.

The present approach promises the greatest amount of success in the shortest time—provided it can succeed at all. And inherent in the present attack upon unnecessary overloading of anxiety is an indirect attack upon the fundamentals of anxiety—or, so it may be. There will not be agreement about this. Sentimental disagreement need not trouble us; such disagreement as will come from serious and competent students of the problem must be considered. At the moment, however, one's view on either side can only be speculative. Time alone can tell. The question is, Will the present approach tend to solve the problem of high anxiety-potential by bringing to a minimum those psychological factors within the growing child that lead to anxiety, or will a wholly new set of factors be created that may be no better than the old? Will a totally new condition be produced or will new problems merely replace the old ones?

The indirect attack lies in the freedom of the parents and the children from the home. That our emotionally overheated homes produce the factors that create anxiety there can be little doubt. What will happen in a completely aerated home? Not in drafty or even gusty homes such as we often see here, but in homes hygienically aerated; in homes where the home is a rich part of the life of the father and mother, but not the whole life; where the children are welcomed and represent something for which there could be no substitute, but do not represent everything; where children can feel that they belong, but not exclusively; where children will have a loyalty, but not a total loyalty, probably not even a first loyalty.

That something of psychological importance will happen we can well believe; that it will be for good there is certainly reason for believing; that it may carry with it other kinds of seed there may possibly be reason for believing; that it is an experiment worth trying surely no informed person would deny. And this experiment must come about as it is inherent in the social changes that have to do with the relief of anxiety-overloading.

These generalizations of mine were not what I applied readymade to the situation. They came only haltingly after much baffling exploration. Let me retrace my steps.

I went to Russia not differentiating particularly between psychiatry, social psychiatry and mental hygiene. I went thinking in terms of hospitals, outpatient clinics, schools for the feebleminded, special classes in the public schools; of clinics in correctional institutions, clinics in the courts (particularly juvenile), clinics in social agencies, community clinics; of psychiatric social work, modern types of training in mental-hygiene personnel, psychiatrists, psychologists and psychiatric social workers; and finally of child-guidance clinics, mental-hygiene clinics in schools and colleges, vocational guidance, personnel work in industry, teacher and parental training.

I arrived and went to work. First inquiry: Have they this type of organization and that? Yes. And how many of each? So and so many. Not particularly impressive. And how many patients visit the clinic in a day, a month, a year? So and so. Nothing special. Psychiatrists at the courts? Yes. All prisoners examined before trial or before sentence? No. What per cent? Apparently not quite as well as we are doing.

Alcoholic Preventorium. The usual questions as to number of patients, length of stay, method of admission and finally—results? Fifty to sixty per cent. What! Well, here *is* something! Fifty to sixty per cent recovery—and after how long? Six months. And what happens after six months? They all do well. You follow them for how long? Six months. But how then do you know what happens after six months? Oh, we are sure they all do well—or at least most of them. You hope they do, but how can you know? Oh, we feel quite sure. Well, that's that, and it doesn't look very good.

The Prophylactorium for Prostitutes. The same questions and in the end the same answer—sure that everything is well without follow-up data that could make it possible to know. And so through all the range of psychiatric and mental-hygiene organizations; note-book pages filled with questions and answers.

I noted a restlessness at times as I persisted, particularly if I were driving home questions that tended to expose possible inadequacies or to reveal an actual lack of facts in support of certain confident assertions. Sometimes, particularly when dealing with a younger untravelled official, inexperienced in dealing with foreigners, I noted a certain bewilderment on his part. Why all these questions? What were they trying to get at? But everyone was polite and kindly and willing no end to be of service and get whatever information was wanted even though they couldn't understand what reason there was for it all.

And certainly a dozen times I had been asked if I did not want to visit the Museum of the Revolution, the Park of Culture and Rest, a factory, a public kitchen. Propaganda? Was this to distract one's attention from what one was here to do—the gathering of facts in regard to mental hygiene in Russia? But I had always politely declined; refused to be dragged away from the job and to be filled up with propaganda. " If there is time later I shall be delighted to see those things but now I must visit hospitals and clinics."

And so, after inquiry and orientation, visitation. Hospital. Good average, clean, not too crowded, a beginning of occupational therapy. Number of patients to physicians, nurses? Not bad. Training of the nurse, psychiatrist? Sounds a bit inadequate. Out-patient department? No. Social workers? Yes. There is a great deal of talk about social work but it all seems a bit vague.

There is a department for children here. Two hundred of them—two hundred insane children? What in the world can that mean? Let's get there as quickly as possible. Ages? Eight to eighteen. Feeble minded? A few, not many. Then what? These are manic-depressive, these epileptic, these dementia præcox. Shades of German psychiatry! Here is a special section —for disturbed dementia præcox; a hallway with small rooms at either side, what in the old days we would have called " strong " rooms for disturbed patients. A lad of nine in his nightgown stands by his bed crying. He talks readily to our motherly interpreter—she has two of her own—and why does he cry? He wants to go home; he wants his mother and his brothers.

We continue through the wards. It is early afternoon of a pleasant autumn day. It is the rest hour and every child is in bed. None is asleep but all are in bed resting, the manic-depressives here and the dementia præcox there. Also the psychopathic personalities and the constitutional psychopathic inferiors. Mental hygiene in Russia! One wishes that in some miraculous way one could waft Stevenson and Lowrey and Kenworthy and

Thom and Levy and a few motor-car loads of their assistants over here to clean out this place. It should be said, however, that on the physical side these children were receiving excellent care.

But if we can possibly get a toe-hold on a tram we must proceed to the prison and perhaps there we will find evidence of mental hygiene.

But every doctor, every psychologist—it would seem almost every nurse, if not some of the patients, even the eight-year-olds—has asked us if we have seen or if we would not like to visit the Museum of the Revolution, the Park of Culture and Rest, a factory, a food kitchen. This eternal propaganda! And it's all through the hospital—busts and pictures of Lenin and Karl Marx, every ward organized on a communistic basis with its chosen leader, again even to the eight-year-olds, each ward with its classes in socialism, each with its communistic paper prepared by the patients (hand-lettering on large manilla sheets) and fastened upon the wall.

The prison for women. Psychiatrists? Yes, but none is at the prison at the moment. All examined? Yes, it is believed so. Much abnormality found? No, not much, only occasionally. Psychologists? Yes, our informant is the psychologist. Intelligent tests? Y-e-s, with little enthusiasm. What is the average intellectual age? Oh, they are practically all normal; a few mental defectives, perhaps. How many? Not many. And your duties? Education. Reading and writing and the like? A little, not much; there are a large number of illiterates; these are organized into classes and taught by others. And your duties? Educational—which turns out to be teaching Communism. Social work? Yes, again very vague. Method of treatment? Occupational teaching, self-government and " education ". Results? Good. Follow-up? Not much—but have you visited the Museum of the Revolution, the Park of Culture and Rest, a factory, a public kitchen ! ! !

Days of this—and yet, where is the mental hygiene? One has found the usual sort of thing : hospital, special school, clinic; one has met psychiatrists, psychologists, pedologists and has heard much of social work. But one has found nothing exceptional. Good organization, good work here and there as it might be found anywhere. But certainly nothing worth travelling six thousands of miles to see.

And yet I was not discouraged, though I ached with the exertion of it all, this running about in a city with practically no taxis and too few trams. Weary and with nothing as reward I should have been discouraged. But I was not; nor did I regret that I had come. I was glad that I had come. There *is* mental hygiene here. There is something to *learn*. One is somehow aware of this. But what and where is it?

In a queer sort of way there is " mental hygiene " all over the place. There is something different about the crowds on the street; there is something different about the jams in the trams, about the patients in the hospitals, the convicts in the prisons, the children in the special schools. And with the professional people with whom I had talked—why were they a bit puzzled by all my questions, why were they not discouraged and a bit embarrassed at having to give so many negative or compromising answers? They should have been. But they weren't particularly; there was a something in them beyond these questions ; there was an assurance and confidence in them that was not disturbed by their negative answers.

Dirt.  I got the first clue to what I was seeking through dirt.

These people are dirty !  Frightfully dirty !  Did one ever see such hordes of shabby people, hordes that jam the smaller streets and swarm over the larger squares at all times of day and late into the night.  And such people—bedraggled, patched and dirty.  It is oppressive.  But dirty ?  Frightfully dirty !  Wait—an idea—the first ray of light.  How about those trams ?

For days I have been riding miles upon miles in those trams.  It has been cool, sometimes rainy, so that the windows have been closed.  For a half-hour at a time I have been spread like a paste through those trams.  No sardine box ever was so full as a Moscow tram ; by comparison the underground at the rush hour is like a football match with the stands half empty.  One is indeed a floating spirit.  One's legs may be anywhere, one is not sure where they have gone.  The only member one is aware of is the arm and hand with which one is clutching at someone.  The other arm has floated off somewhere and one can only hope that it will return eventually with the legs.  The solidity one feels around the middle, is it the lady's buttocks or one's own stomach, and behind is it one's own buttocks or someone else's stomach ?  It does not really matter ; for the moment we are just one solid body.  Windows closed, scarcely enough air to breathe—and yet I was not ill ; odours that should have turned one's stomach were not there.  (Others report differently, I know.  But I wonder.  I can only report my own experience and what, as a shock, it revealed to me about myself.  Later, on inquiry, I

learned that every section of the city has several community bath-houses and that they are popular and much
used.)

Because these people ought to be dirty, by my standards, they were dirty.  Nowhere, in America, could one
find so many people on the street dressed so shabbily—
not in the worst sections of our cities.  Such clothes mean
dirt.  Clothes twice as good would mean dirt and much
dirt in America.  Therefore they must mean dirt in
Russia.  But they didn't—and that was my clue.

I would have sworn I had come to Russia open-minded,
even hopefully, and ready to learn.  But I had brought
a plan, a system, an ideology with me.  I had brought
measuring-rods with which I was familiar.  I thought I
knew what I was to look for and how I was to judge
it when I found it.  I had gone to Russia as I might
have gone to some other part of my own country to make
a " survey ".  Although unaware of it, I had gone to
Russia to see how much of *our* idea they had absorbed
rather than to find out what *their* idea might be and how
they were working it out and with what success.

Had I visited the Museum of the Revolution, the Park
of Culture and Rest, a factory, a community kitchen ?

Perhaps at the risk of being innoculated with propaganda it would be well to let the Russians tell me what
is in their minds rather than for me to propagandize
myself by collecting information on the hooks of my
questionable questions.

How do the Russians conceive mental hygiene and
how are they working out mental-hygiene problems in
accordance with their conceptions ?  Another thought
occurs at this time : we have long held that these things
—hospitals, special schools and classes, court and prison

clinics and the like, important social undertakings in themselves—are not " mental hygiene " ; that they have come to be thought of as mental hygiene because their activities have been carried on under that name ; but that mental hygiene must have to do with *keeping well people well*, of so organizing life and the emotional develop- ment of the individual that the anxieties and fears that lead to defensive reactions on his part and which end in inefficiency, unhappiness and often illness and anti-social conduct, be minimized so that he may be in a position to contribute of his best.   Is it possible that this idea, which has such feeble recognition in the West, where our energy goes so preponderately into the rehabilitation of the perhaps ten to fifteen per cent of the population that has got into difficulty—in our efforts to solve the " crime " problem, the " problem of the feebleminded " and half a dozen other " problems "—is it possible that Russia is thinking in terms of one hundred per cent of the popu- lation, of mental hygiene in a positive instead of a nega- tive sense ?

Rosenstein (director of the State Institute for Mental Hygiene in Moscow) drops a remark.   " The difference between mental hygiene in Russia and America," he says, " is that in America you have propaganda *about* mental hygiene and excellent work with individuals in your child-guidance clinics and clinics in the schools and colleges, while in Russia we have *mental hygiene* propa- ganda and our work is with the mass rather than with the individual."

He has put it in a nutshell ; and it is the thing for which we have been fumbling for days.   Now comes some light on why our questions were regarded with such bewilderment and why we were so frequently asked if we had seen the Museum of Revolution, the Park of Culture and Rest, a factory, a community kitchen.   What we were asking about was not mental hygiene, except of a sort ; these other things were mental hygiene.   Why were we bothering with the one and paying no attention to the other ?

So it was that I came to see that the difference between mental hygiene in America and mental hygiene in Russia is the difference between life, or the philosophy of life, in America, and life, or the philosophy of life, in Russia.   As I said at the beginning, in America we live in a democracy, with equal opportunity for all and personal progress dependent upon the success of our competition with others.   In Russia one lives not in a communistic state, but in a state in the process of building a civilization based upon communism, where the individual is important but as a part of the group, and the group is important but only in the sense that it is made up of individuals.   The two are the same thing.   I am an individual but I am the group ; I am the group but I am an individual.   There is only one loyalty—to the group, but that is myself ; or to myself, but that is the group. This sounds simple enough, but what follows logically from it is not so easily grasped.   It is, however, fundamental and nothing is to be understood in Russia until this is understood.   Our difficulty in understanding it is because here we have nothing comparable.   One has a loyalty here not to *a* group but to *many* groups and as the interests of these various groups often come into conflict, conflict arises within us.

The first step in Russian mental hygiene, therefore, is the emphasis upon the worth-whileness of the individual —this may sound strange to many who have read about

Russia—and the importance of what happens to the individual.

In a programme, as I outlined it earlier in this chapter, so general as to coincide practically with a social programme, what is the function of the psychiatrist or the psychologist ?

To the limit of their personnel he is in the school, the prison, the court, the special agency, the *factory*, as here. But with this important difference.  He is much interested in the individual who has become ill or maladjusted in his situation (as we are) and uses his best skill and the facilities at his command in recovering that individual —for that individual is important ; the difference between illness and health is the difference between an effective and an ineffective.  But that is not all of his function. His most important function is to see to it that the methods and procedure in the school, the prison, the agency, the *factory*, are such as to build up the mental health of those engaged there rather than to injure or destroy it.  What a crazy idea !  What a crazy place !

The school, the social agency, the prison, the clinic, the factory do not exist in and of themselves, each with an independent programme.  The school is not just providing " culture ", the social agency " relief ", the court " justice ", the prison " reform ", the clinic " adjustment ", the factory stockings.  There are not six programmes here.  There is but one programme.  There is, therefore, no artificial antagonism between the psychiatrist and the principal of the school, the warden of the prison, the foreman of the factory,  Each has the same objective—their part (school, agency, prison, factory) in the whole programme (the one general programme). There is but one question, therefore : How can we gain our objective, that is, contribute our part to the whole ? In other words, again, unified activity not co-operative activity, and a unity of activity that obtains both within an organization and between organizations.

It all sounds a bit fantastic, like a world gone mad. Who ever heard of human beings behaving like that ? But the most fantastic part of it all is that it is actually in process, although not accomplished, to be sure, among one hundred and sixty millions of people spread over a third of the earth's surface. And the greatest fraud of all is that it would seem to be nothing but the commonest kind of common sense. So common that one wonders how one could have been so fooled.

# CHAPTER II

## RUSSIA: A NATION OF ADOLESCENTS

OF the many misconceptions in regard to Russia, three seem to me of special importance :

That what is happening in Russia is exceedingly complicated and therefore difficult to understand ;

That Russia is engaged in an industrial revolution ;

That the Russians are realists of the hardest and cruelest type.

What has happened in Russia is quite simple. They have got rid of God. They have taken upon themselves the responsibility of understanding and organizing their world. Getting rid of God means, of course, merely getting rid of God-priest ideology and all its supernatural ramifications—it in no way limits the potentialities of the individual for human fellowship. Murky-mindedness melts like snow before the sun.

The revolution in Russia is essentially not industrial, but spiritual. The industrial side is merely an incident, a means to an end. It looms large at present and it is important, but behind it is something more important. Russia is probably the only country in the world to-day that has a significant spiritual life.

The Russians themselves disavow with scorn " capitalistic idealism " and choose to call themselves " dialectical materialists ". They are materialists of the realest sort —up to a point. Nowhere are physical or social problems

16

approached with such realism—at least up to a point.
That point in each instance is the limit of *their* knowledge ; not necessarily the limit of knowledge—but the
extent of their present thinking. That their realism stops
at this point is understandable  But then what ?  Realism
would demand a halt, an admission of the end of the
road, the formulation of further investigation along
realistic lines in order to discover new trails that might
lead somewhere. In certain fields, physical, chemical,
this is done. In the social and human field the Russian
at this point somersaults into an idealism for which there
is scarcely a counterpart in " capitalism ", an idealism
that becomes naïveté. In spite of his scorn of " idealism ", he acts as an idealist, but an idealist whose realism
saves him from sentimentality.

One explanation may lie in the " psychology " which
the revolutionary leaders studied before the Revolution
as they studied everything else. Lenin is said to have had
more than three hundred men and women trained in
various professions in the European universities, ready
for special responsibilities. This preparation was going
on during a period when " psychology " scarcely existed.
Such psychology as there was consisted either of philosophical discussions about the " will ", " emotion " and
the like, or of nervous physiology. What there was the
revolutionary leaders devoured line by line, but through
no fault of their own their knowledge of " psychology "
was far less, and is to-day far less, than of any other field.
They were forced to a psychological idealism because
they had no other psychology with which to work.
Fortunately for them it is an idealism not wholly unjusti-
fied, but it has its limitation. As the limit becomes clear—
and with their searching self-criticism, like nothing in the

world, they will be quick to see it—they will, no doubt, become as realistic in psychology as in electro-dynamics.

"Ah," but someone says, " how I wish I had their lack of knowledge if I could be as successful at putting something over."

The writer of a recent article in *The* (*New York*) *Nation's* series, " If I were Dictator ", remarked that among other things he would send a commission to Russia to study their psychological methods.   Not a bad idea : there is much to learn.   But our friend is confusing psychology with " salesmanship " and guides advertised under that name for " putting one's self across ".   The " psychology " that has worked in Russia is the simplest in the world—show by what you do that you mean what you say.

The question as to whether the Russian is an " idealist " or " realist "—to oppose the two, for the moment begging the question of a combination—is not merely academic ; it has important implications for mental hygiene.   Up to a point the Russians handle a maladjusted individual with the best realism.   When this succeeds, well and good. When it fails—then they are stumped.   The curious part is that at the point where we are idealists if not sentimentalists, they are realists ;  and at the point where they become idealists we do our best work as realists.   We sentimentalize a great deal about the individual, his potentialities, his sacred person, his freedom, his opportunity—at this point we are thorough idealists—then we turn him loose to devour or be devoured.   After he has been thoroughly mauled and beaten up we become realists and in the best realistic fashion examine *him* to find out what is the matter with *him* that he has got all out of " adjustment ".

While we are sentimentalizing about the individual
the Russians are asserting *that the individual is important*
and that he *shall* have an opportunity to develop his
potentialities.    Here they would assert that they are not
idealists, but realists.    If the individual becomes " maladjusted " (the point at which we become at least partially
realists) the Russian tries to blind himself to the fact
that there might actually be something wrong with the
individual himself, insists that he is quite all right and
that more of the same social medicine will cure him.    If
in the end—and they are patient beyond words—the
individual does not (cannot, and for definite reasons, as
our realism would say) adjust, then there is sharp, quick
action and off he goes to life in some permanent quarters.
Not as a punishment (by which they have recognized
what they have tended to deny) but as one who will
not or cannot, for reasons beyond reach (which is not
true in many instances), pull his load in the boat.

And yet the Russians are quite right in the method
they are pursuing at the moment—provided they do not
deceive themselves—as a straightforward realistic policy
in the face of a definite situation.    The vastness of the
undertaking in Russia and the speed with which many
things must be accomplished preclude spending too much
time over unpromising material.    Russia's job at the
moment is to find, prepare and get into action her effectives.    She is right in assuming that the great majority of
her one hundred and sixty million are capable of being
effective, given proper opportunity ; she is further right
in believing that the great majority of her delinquents,
prostitutes and other social parasites, most of whom have
had no opportunity, are also capable of becoming social
effectives.    The Russians would insist that this was

equally true in any of the Western countries. Admitting this in part, on the whole one would have to deny it. In the winnowing process now going on in Russia there will be a residue—there is already a residue. Russia will find, as others have found by methods as realistic as any used in solving electrical problems, that there are individual differences which must be taken into account in the last analysis. That there exists a greater equality of potentiality than shows up in any " capitalistic " country, one would grant at once ; and also that many of the " differences " in capitalistic countries are artificially created by a combination of sentimentality and cruelty. But not all. One will watch with the greatest interest to see if the Russian system—the totality of ideology and plan—does not create a greater equality by diminishing the number of " differences ". But differences there will be : a future problem which Russians no doubt will eventually attack as realistically as they now attack other problems.

Having decided to organize their own lives and having set a goal—the Communist State—the Russians have not fumbled and staggered toward this ideal bearing banners and shouting slogans. Planned activity, as the world knows, is the key to their progress.

Outside of Russia one hears mostly of the industrial planning. The Five-Year Plan has become almost synonymous with that part of the total plan which involves industry. Planning, however, involves every activity within the nation, even to the work of a research student in one of the many scientific institutes. Things are not left to individual inspiration or mood or voluntary co-operation. To contemplate the thinking that has gone on in working out the details of these plans gives one a headache. Amazing common sense has been used in emphasis and proportion, putting first things first, submerging professional pride and bumptiousness.  Examining the strides that have been made in carrying out the plan, knowing with what human material it has had to be done in the face of difficulties such as lack of training, and gross illiteracy, knowing, too, how infinitely lesser plans fail in our own country with personnel trained presumably to the last minute, one becomes thoughtful.

These plans are not superimposed from above.  They are worked out from below, co-ordinated, promulgated and directed from above—but with responsibility for carrying out below.  The plan begins and ends with the individual and each individual can feel his responsibility at both points.[1]

The printed plan for medicine consists of a volume of several hundred pages.  What are the needs—country, village, city, nation ; what is the order of importance of these needs ; what have we to meet these needs ; how can this best be distributed ; what are the minimal needs at any one point ; what can be done at once to meet this minimal need ; in five years can we have the situation in hand—no ; what may we reasonably expect ; what is the first series of steps, the second, the third ; roughly what should we be looking forward to in the second five-year period, the third ?

Similar plans exist in nursing, teaching, housing, cooking, the so-called " social problems ", in every activity. And these are not isolated plans, a nursing plan growing up parallel and antagonistic to a medical plan with smiling

[1] For an excellent account of the steps in preparation and method of administration of a " plan " (coal industry) see, "Observations on Management in the Soviet Union ", by Mary Van Kleeck, Director of Social Studies, Russell Sage Foundation, New York, *Taylor Society Bulletin*, April, 1933.

" co-operation " on the outside and bitterness on the inside, or a teaching plan growing side by side with other social activities but with a wall around it through which one may pass only as an intruder.  Physician, nurse, educator, social worker are building Communism.  Their pride is not in their person, their position, their profession but in what as individuals, professional or non-professional, they can contribute to the one undertaking that has meaning for them all.  This is true also of artists, dramatists, musicians, writers ;  it explains why so much that they do appears to us as " propaganda ".  To them Communist subjects are as natural an expression as trees or the Volga and they are mystified by our use of the word " propaganda ".

When we come to the scientists mocking at " pure science ", " capitalistic science ", and establishing Red Institutes to make Red Science we are stumped for a moment—a good many members of the International Psycho-technical Congress that met in Moscow at the time of my first visit were left gnashing their teeth and spluttering—but it is best to count ten, if not a hundred, before starting to splutter.  A fact is still a fact in Russia, but for the moment the Russian scientist would like to know where the fact belongs in the order of facts before he gets too excited about it.  Facts, like everything else at this critical time, have got to " behave ".  The scientist too is building Communism.  Since he is building it realistically, he has a tremendous respect for facts.  He has no desire to deny facts ;  he intends to use every one. If you think otherwise, take him for a fool and try to ask him a few simple questions that will go to the heart of the matter and bring down his house like a stack of cards—you will burn your fingers a nice bright red.

This attitude toward science, facts, what you will, has frequently been compared to " Catholic Science " or " Methodist Science " and, as it is agreed that there can be no such thing, it is assumed that there cannot be a " Red Science ".   True enough, in that sense, but a little investigation will show that the Russian scientist holds equally as ridiculous any special science and that he, too, does not wish to prejudice facts by any standard other than scientific.  The fact scientifically established becomes a part of life and the question becomes how can that fact be used in the undertaking now in hand ?

The medical organization in Moscow can be taken as an example of the type that is being worked out in all parts of Russia, though still far from being realized throughout the country.   Moscow is divided into fourteen districts.   Each district is covered with a network of community clinics leading usually from a central district clinic through neighbourhood clinics to the factories, the schools and other institutions within the district.   Lines in the other direction lead from the central clinic to the hospitals, general and special, located in Moscow and its environs.   Passage up and down these lines is easy.   The organization functions as a whole, not as a loosely joined series of clinics and hospitals, each jealous and ambitious, but " co-operative ".   An individual can be passed efficiently through this entire chain from factory, home, school to hospital if that is necessary, or his needs can be attended to at various points in the chain if that is all that is required.   The aim is efficient and prompt treatment of *anyone* who is ill, to the full extent of his need ; the restoration of the individual's effectiveness as quickly as can be done with safety ; the teaching of hygiene and the prevention of illness.

The central clinic in each district is a large organization equipped not only for general medicine but for the handling of special problems. The neighbourhood clinic is naturally smaller and devoted to general medicine and the specialties most likely to be needed. From all clinics both general clinicians and specialists are " on call " to visit the sick in their homes. In addition to psychiatrists daily " on call " at the clinics there are two psychiatrists " on call " during the night.

The work and plans of the Ordinka Street General Prophylactic Dispensary in the name of Professor Rein in the Lenin District of Moscow are good examples of community-clinic organization and planning. In this district there are sixty neighbourhood clinics. In 1927–28 when the clinic was organized there were thirty-three. These were increased to thirty-eight in 1929, to forty-seven in 1930 and the plan calls for a further increase in 1932 to seventy and in 1933 to eighty. In 1929 there were eighty general physicians visiting in the homes from this clinic ; in 1930, one hundred ; 1931, one hundred and thirty ; the plan calls for an increase to one hundred and sixty during 1932–33. In 1929–30 the pediatricians on the staff were increased to thirty-one. The number was increased in 1931 to thirty-six. The plan calls for forty-two in 1932 and forty-six in 1933. In 1933 the staff is to consist of more than two hundred and thirty-six physicians, one hundred and sixty general, forty-six pediatricians, twenty tuberculosis specialists for adults and ten for children, with the addition of neurologists and psychiatrists, gynæcologists, ear, nose, and throat specialists, and so on. There are at the present time eight neurologists and psychiatrists on duty at this clinic, with plans for doubling this number. The plan for this

district calls for a medical unit for each factory employ-
ing four hundred or more workers ; for smaller factories,
a nurse first-aid unit.

There is a clinic surprising for a factory at the Red
Flag Textile works in Leningrad where seven thousand
five hundred workers are employed.  This clinic was open
daily from 10 a.m. to 7.30 p.m.  In addition to the department for internal medicine it has departments for surgery, women, eye, psychiatry and neurology, ear-nose-
throat and dentistry.  During the month of July there
had been five hundred and fifty-seven total visits to the
department of neurology and psychiatry with fifty new
cases.  Of these fifty, forty-one were unable to work and
had been sent to hospitals, sanitaria or rest homes or
were returning from their homes to the clinic for treatment—with no loss in pay.  This department has a ten-
bed ward at the factory equipped for electro-, helio- and
physio-therapy.[1]

The mental-hygiene activities of Russia are headed up
in the State Scientific Institute for Neuro-Psychiatric Prophylaxis of which Dr. L. Rosenstein is the director.  The
Institute consists of a polyclinic for nervous and mental
diseases and a research department with bureaux for
mental-hygiene education, neurology, mental hygiene,
community organizations and psycho-technics.  The
work of the Institute reaches to the factories, the colleges,
the Red Army, the Houses of Culture, the Workers'

[1] For a more complete account of medical aims and organiz-
ation in Russia see *Red Medicine : Socialized Health in Soviet
Russia*, by Sir Arthur Newsholme and John A. Kingsbury.
London : Heinemann, 1934.  See also " Medical and Other
Conditions in Soviet Russia ", *The Scientific Monthly*, July,
1932, and " Socialized Medicine in the Soviet Union ", *Soviet
Russia Today*, April, 1934, by Lewellys F. Barker, M.D.

Clubs, courts and prisons, the general dispensaries ; the various scientific and medical institutes, such as the Institute for Motherhood and Childhood, the Prophy- lactoria for Prostitution, the Hospital for Alcoholics ; the postgraduate courses in the medical schools and colleges, and the mental hospitals. Occupational therapy is being rapidly developed in the mental hospitals. The plan, however, is not for occupational therapy departments within the hospital, except for minor things, but work in factories in the surrounding community. Dr. Rosen- stein is directly responsible to the commissioner of public health who has under his direction all provision for the sick with the exception of the railway workers.

In addition to the Psychopathic Department of the Hospital for Mental Disease of the Moscow University I, long famous among the world's psychiatric hospitals, an excellent new hospital, the Psychopathic Hospital in the name of Soloviov, the " first step in Soviet psychiatry ", has been built in connection with Moscow University II. The hospital is built on the grounds of the former Dun- skaya military hospital. It was established in 1920 and consists of one hundred and seventy beds for adults and fifty beds for children.

But one cannot learn of mental hygiene by studying organization. Organization is but a skeleton and may mean much or little. An elaborate clinic planted in a court may look well on a chart, but if the atmosphere of the court is permeated with all that is mentally unhealthy it has little significance. We can better sense Russia's work in mental hygiene by examining a few special activities.

" Liquidation " is a popular word in Russia. The Russians like to define a problem, isolate it, and then

" liquidate " it.   In " liquidating " a problem a definite
step-by-step programme is prepared such as one might
prepare for a military campaign.   The problem of the
" wild boys ", the orphans of soldiers and of parents
killed in the Revolution, who in the middle 1920's
prowled the city streets and country-side waiting for prey,
has been " liquidated ".   At least a part of the story is
told in the film, *The Road to Life*, which has been shown
in Britain and the United States.

Prostitution and alcoholism are two problems now being
actively worked upon.   To discuss in detail the work
of the Prophylactoria for Prostitution or the Hospital
for Alcoholics, or the courts or the schools would carry
us too far for our present purpose, but we may examine
some of the mental-hygiene features in these institutions.
We shall find plenty of mental hygiene but not of our
sort.   We shall not find a single clinic ; there are no psychologists at the Prophylactoria for Prostitution although
psychiatrists call regularly for the examination of special
cases ; psychiatrists and psychologists are available at the
court but not for routine work.   The mental hygiene in
the court comes from the bench, not from a special room
down some corridor ; the mental hygiene in the school
from the instructors, not from a " guidance clinic " in the
basement.

At the time of the Revolution there were said to have
been twenty-five thousand registered prostitutes in Moscow.   Immediately after the Revolution prostitution was
made illegal by decree and prostitutes were no longer
registered.   In 1924 when the first Prophylactorium for
Prostitution was organized (by 1931 there were five in
Moscow and many others throughout the Union) it was
estimated that there were five thousand prostitutes in

Moscow; by 1928 this estimate had dropped to three thousand and it is now believed that there are not more than four hundred to five hundred. It is expected that the problem will be " liquidated " within the next two years. Yes—really; and personally I should not be surprised.

In this " liquidation " many factors are at work, important among them the organized efforts of the prophylactoria. The workers at the head of the prophylactoria would be surprised to hear their work called mental hygiene, but what else is it? It doesn't consist of psychological and psychiatric examinations or case studies, in our sense. It consists in teaching the girl that she has a place in the scheme of things; that she is the only one who feels that she is unimportant and no good; that she not only has a place but that she is wanted, in fact, needed in that place; that friendship, marriage, children, study if she is interested, leadership, are all possible for her if she will but take her place. (And this is no hoax, it is actually true.) To that end she must learn to read and write and become a " qualified worker ", that is, one trained in some pursuit. Qualified, she must work, at present seven hours a day, four days in five (1931). The institution is prepared to give her the necessary instruction; during her period of learning she will receive all necessary medical care, food and lodging and a small amount of money. She will be trained to use the modern machines that she will find when she leaves the institution and enters the factory as a " qualified worker ". The mental hygiene in all this—the best in the world—is security, present and future; purpose, sense of belonging, sense of being needed, sense of personal worth and value as a human being; confidence in herself, in others and in the joint activity ; consciousness of opportunity, freedom from fear. What is this but what we attempt to attain stripped of our terms—ego, libido, sublimation and the like—and our elaborate paraphernalia ? With all the trained personnel and clinical equipment that we could conceivably bring together could we by our method in our social organization attain as much ? Are we hindered by our method or our social organization ? We shall come to face this question.

Alcoholism is a serious problem in Russia. An intensive campaign of education is waged against alcohol and a quite active one against tobacco as well. By placards, pamphlets, books, lectures this campaign is carried on wherever workers meet, most actively perhaps in the schools and among the organization for Communist youths. It is not a " moral " campaign in our sense ; it has nothing of religious salvation in it. It is a campaign for a clear head free of narcotic befuddlement of any kind, whether religion, alcohol or opium.

Drunkenness, it is claimed, has been much reduced ; the group feeling mounts strongly against it and it is easy to see why, since every person who cannot work because of drunkenness has to be carried by those who are sober and work. The worker doesn't pay indirectly by having his prices raised because of the " charity " the head of the factory has given for the care of alcoholics. He pays directly and he knows it. In the courtyard of a factory one often sees a wooden structure in the form of a large vodka bottle. The worker who has lost time through drunkenness cannot get his pay at the end of the week from the cashier's window with the others. He receives his money in the courtyard before the others from the window in the vodka bottle. These bottles have on them various inscriptions, all different ways of saying " Shame Money " or " Shameful Money ". It is no joke for the worker.

But what happens to an alcoholic ?

You will find him perhaps lying in the mud in the middle of the street.

But we must begin with the policeman who will come to get the man, for the policeman is like something that never was before in Heaven or on earth. It's simple, like so many things in Russia. *He's a citizen.* Just a citizen ; only his job is to keep order while someone else's job is to run a stocking machine or to cart bricks. He wears a uniform but it is just a different kind of work-clothes. You sit by him in the opera—there are dozens of him there in the audience, perhaps alone, perhaps with his best girl or his family. If you are lucky you may sit with him in his club, for the policeman has his club as does the writer and the artist—not a barracks or a " stationhouse " but a well-appointed club, for himself, his wife and his children.

The Moscow " cop " with whom I talked most, as we sat drinking tea in his club, was interested to know what operas were given at the Metropolitan in New York ; had I heard Chaliapin, what were our best symphonic orchestras, and about George Gershwin and Broadway ? It all seemed quite natural until one realized that one was drinking tea and talking music with a " cop ". This particular cop was exceptional, certainly, but there was no reason to believe that the others I met at that club were unusual—handsome, well set up, intelligent, friendly, keenly interested to hear about America and to tell about Russia.

It is a chap like this who carts away the citizen lying

in the mud. To jail ? No ; to a semi-hospital where he is examined by a physician and treated if necessary ; washed up and put into a clean bed. After he comes to he remains a few days until he gets on his legs. During this time " education " begins.

The alcoholic is likely to be in about the same situation as the prostitute, a peasant who has wandered into the city, ignorant, illiterate, without a trade, befuddled by the life about him and his inability to get in step. " Education " again consists in showing him what he needs in order to get on ; in convincing him that no one is pulling his leg with beautiful talk but that he is wanted, needed ; that an opportunity is his if he desires it. The first lessons may be enough, with assistance to a job or to training. If he doesn't grasp this, sooner or later he is returned. Perhaps for a third time or a fourth. Even yet nobody has bullied him. Patience, patience, patience—" the fellow doesn't yet understand " and on goes the " education ". Here is where the Russian often insists upon being an " idealist " as unreal as any " capitalist " great " social lover ".

Eventually, if it becomes necessary, he will be urged to apply for admission at the Alcoholic Hospital under the direction of Dr. A. Rapaport, a former student of Rosenstein. It is a hospital of one hundred beds, ninety for alcoholics and ten for drugs. The patient comes voluntarily but he must remain for a period of months under active medical therapy combined with more " education " and, as soon as he is ready for it, work in an outside factory. The patient spends three and a half hours daily at the factory, the rest of the time at the hospital undergoing treatments, attending classes in reading or economics and socialism. When the medical staff

believe him able to make the change, he is removed from
the hospital list and entered upon the payroll of the
factory. During the stay in the hospital his wife and
family have received the full wage he had been getting
before his admission.

It does not matter what sort of an institution one
visits—mental hospital, prison, school, court—everywhere that " problems " are to be solved the situation is
the same : not so much special techniques and methods
and personnel as an organized way of life, the very nature
of which increases the morale of the individual, places
a responsibility upon him, and gives him an opportunity
to carry it. The responsibility is not in a sense a personal one—that he must be personally ambitious and
get to the top of the heap—but a responsibility for the
group. Joined with others he helps his group get on ;
that group in turn joined with other groups, helps all
get on. All are definitely going somewhere and they
know where. The individual does not have to worry
about his individuality, his personality, even his " freedom ".

When one speaks of " Russia " of course one does not
speak of everyone in Russia. There is, as a matter of
fact, a surprising unanimity, but it does not include all.
By " Russia " one means the living, vigorous part of
Russia—all else is water over the dam. We may think
what we like about this water and how it got there but
it has no significance in the larger aspect. " Russia "
means to-day those who are building Communism ; those
who are endeavouring to master the physical world and
the mechanics of living in order that there may be an
art of living, a culture, a life for all, useful and satisfying.

The spirit that one finds in Russia is frequently spoken

of as a " war spirit ", a " pioneer spirit ". It is this, certainly, but more. Beneath the hectic, feverish exterior that one sees on superficial view there is among the adults a calmness, a depth and richness of feeling that is something else. It is the spirit of the adolescent in the finest sense. It is all of us when we were at our best, when we were honest, when we saw clearly, when we had faith and courage and goodwill. With our honesty, clear vision, faith, courage and goodwill there was much naïveté, unattached to anything tangible.

Russians are frequently just as naïve in their far-flung visions, their belief in the possibility of everything and the potentiality of everybody, their credulity in what one finds in a book. One is often bewildered ; one comes away from a conference of college professors wondering if one has wandered into an undergraduate discussion. But be very careful ! The utterly, ridiculously impossible has been accomplished in so many instances and is on the very verge of being accomplished in so many more that it is well again to count a hundred before smiling. An amount of sheer youthful naïveté—yes—but mostly the pure metal of adolescence : an adolescence that has idealism but also realism ; that asks questions ; that refuses to accept what has been as an answer ; that wants to know why : an adolescence that is challenged by difficulty ; that does not know the word " impossible " ; does not know when it is beaten. With this and all that it implies directed toward a definite common goal, and with a sixth of the area of the earth in which to expand and experiment—one would like to know the end of the story.[1]

[1] For an excellent discussion of further misunderstandings in regard to Russia see *On Understanding Russia*, by Corliss Lamont, published by Friends of the Soviet Union.

# CHAPTER III

## THE SIGNIFICANCE OF DICTATORSHIP:
### RUSSIA AND ITALY

GRANTED that Italy under Mussolini is a cleaner, more orderly, more efficient country than before and that the people as a whole are happier and healthier—is this the significance of the dictatorship ?

Granted that out of social chaos the dictatorship of the proletariat in Russia has brought an amazing degree of order, has raised to a surprising degree the standard of living for the masses of the people and has changed the state from one of medievalism to a modern industrial state—are these the significant facts of the dictatorship ?

Does dictatorship begin and end in the belly ? Is it entirely a matter of economics ? Has it any other significance ? Is the significance of all dictatorship the same ? At least, is it the same in the case of Italy and Russia ?

In the matter of present results Russia and Italy offer many similarities—orderliness, the obvious improvement in morale of the people generally, the same enthusiasms and loyalties (in Italy, however, for a leader ; in Russia for an idea), an array of " model " institutions, schools, houses, factories. One is soon aware, however, of striking differences and these seem fraught with most important implications for mental hygiene. The differences begin with the type of dictatorship.

Italy's dictatorship is of the kind the world has always

34

known—a powerful man who rules, but with the difference, perhaps, that he ostensibly rules for all, checking
the aggression of the so-called capitalist on the one
hand and the aggression of so-called labour on the other.
Orders, however, are unmistakably from the top.    Individual security is offered provided the individual obeys
orders and loyally supports the leader.

Russia's dictatorship is of a quite different kind.    There
is, indeed, strong authority at the top.    But the orders
that are enforced from the top have in very large part
come up from below.    There is a continuous effort to
pass responsibility to the group.    An extraordinary
amount of thinking is done by the mass as a whole.    It is
not so much a question of following a leader or leaders.
Leaders are for ever saying, " Here is a set of principles ;
think out your problems in the light of them ;    gather
data, discuss, plan.    If you do not know how to read, if
you have too little information, if you do not know how
to make a plan, learn ;    go to those in the community
who can teach you."    The difference is somewhat like that
between an old-fashioned school ruled by a stern school-
master with a rod and a modern " progressive " school.

In Italy the " system " remains the same except that
the more serious aggression are held in check by a
strong hand ;    there is no essential change in social
ideology, in the psychology of the people : no new psychological outlets, no fundamental redirection of energy.
In Russia the " system " has been rooted out ;    a completely new realistic ideology has replaced the old ideology
of superstition, morality and romance ;    new outlets have
been provided for old psychological needs ;    the direction
of energy has been changed.

It is, of course, quite impossible in a single chapter to

discuss all or any considerable number of the differences from the point of view of mental hygiene of these two dictatorships. Perhaps one can get to the heart of the matter by discussing one difference, but one which has ramifications in all directions—the place of women.

In Russia a woman is a human being. In Italy she remains a special creation with a very specialized function. In Russia there is developing an actual equality of women with men. Officially such equality exists ; actually it exists in large and growing part. There is no differentiation of work—men's work and women's work. Work is work and is to be done by whoever likes to do it and can do it best. Every woman works, but not on a double shift—one shift in the office, factory, school, laboratory, or library, and another after returning home. If she works outside the home the work in the home is done for her—not for *her*, which implies a special responsibility, but for the family. It is not a *favour* done her ; it is her right. She has worked as many hours as the husband and if there are dribbles of work left over from the general care it is the husband's responsibility as much as the wife's and he can do his share with no loss of dignity. He has no dignity in this sense to begin with. A woman is economically dependent upon no man. She is dependent upon no man's favours or goodwill. She enters into life as a self-respecting, assured person because nothing can happen to her that will endanger her except such things as may happen to all men.

In Italy there exists no equality between men and women. Women are " superior " to men. Men honour them and are polite, gallant and romantic. But women are dependent upon men's favour and goodwill. A woman has one chief function—child-bearing. She must marry or she does not fulfil her function.    At whatever damage to the integrity of her own personality she must marry the man provided for her or she must find this husband ;  if necessary develop a technique to ensnare him.    Although she knows perfectly well how the marriage was made she must assume that it was sacredly made and that it is indissoluble.    Married, she is entirely dependent for her own life and the life of her children upon the man.    Anxiety, fear enter at the wedding feast with guilt only around the corner to enter as she finds that she is not able to maintain at all times loving, even loyal, thoughts of her husband.    Such security as she may have had within herself becomes undermined and the only security she has is in the Good Father who has promised, not to relieve her of her burdens, but to reward her if she carries them patiently and well ;  in the Virgin Mary who will intercede for her, and various of the saints who have a particular solicitude for mothers.

For she will soon become a mother, as it is her special function and God's will.    The use of contraceptives would be a grievous sin ;  an abortion, possible only at the hands of a criminal, would endanger not only her life but her very soul.    She (not necessarily her husband) will suffer the frustration of continence or she will be a mother many, many times.    If she can repeat the process a sufficient number of times she will win a prize.    The hygienic implications here as to what all this means in the psychological development of the woman are too obvious to warrant discussion.    At no time from earliest childhood to adolescence, from adolescence through womanhood, from womanhood to death can she be self-reliant, can she be honest, think her own thoughts, recognize her own desires.    Always there must be denial, dissimulation, dishonesty—all destructive of psychological integrity—or heavy penalties in guilts, anxiety and fear —equally destructive. No change in this degradation of women in the name of duty and beauty has been made by the dictatorship. The emotional and spiritual (not in the sense of church) development of children, broods of them, rests in the hands of those whose chief outlet for distorted emotions those children must themselves be. A culture-bed for future aggression could not be better prepared if it were under glass.

In Russia an economically free, self-respecting woman joins her life with an equally economically free and self-respecting man. They do so of their own free will. It is a joint enterprise entered into for mutual content, happiness and the rearing of a family. They are " in love ". They enjoy being in love. But they are not over-burdened with illusions in regard to " love ". They have probably been in love before and they have probably consummated such love experiences. Being in love is a beautiful experience but they do not hold it sacred ; the romanticism may not long endure ; they are prepared for it going, knowing that as they continue to grow other values may take its place. Knowing all this they enter into their relationship without fear or anxiety, hoping that it will mean continued growth and development for both of them but knowing, too, that if it doesn't it can easily be dissolved. If the marriage does not bring mutual satisfaction and growth then it not only serves no purpose but becomes destructive. It will be dissolved by mutual consent, or if bitterness has entered in one will ask for a divorce and it will be granted for the asking. The question as to why a divorce is desired will not even be raised. It is enough that it is desired. If there are children, provision will be made for their care until they are eighteen years of age.

The marriage and divorce bureau are in the same room. In fact marriages are registered and divorces granted at the same table by the same person, a young woman whom we would regard as a social worker. On the table are two books, one for marriages, one for divorces. Perhaps the first applicant is a young man who asks for a divorce. It is granted as soon as certain data as to name, age, and the like can be recorded. No reasons are asked. The young man is followed by a series of healthy, obviously happy young men and women, the girls about eighteen, the boys twenty, desiring to be married. This is accomplished, too, in the time that it takes to record certain data. Then, a young woman applies for a divorce. And so it goes throughout the day, dignified but pleasant, none of the hushed quiet of sanctity, nothing of the heavy hand of fate, no tragedy or dramatics, no ribaldry. Amusement at times as when the clerk picks up the wrong book or, as on one occasion, towards the end of a morning, a tragi-comedy from an old stage. A gaunt, distressed-looking woman rushing into the room began to shout excitedly as soon as she had crossed the threshold of the door, " I want a divorce ! I want a divorce ! I'm fifty years old, my husband is sixty-five. He drinks all the time and won't leave other women alone." She seemed to feel that she must fight for what she wanted, defend and justify herself, prove her assertions—so that it was difficult for the clerk to quiet her sufficiently to get the few statistical items that she wanted. And the constant emphasis upon the difference in ages and the fact that the husband was " not satisfied with one woman " showed the confusion in her own mind, as indeed there was in her effort to pass from the medievalism of her youth to the life of to-day. A chapter from an old book !

In the ordinary course of events there will be children in the home. But the children will come as wanted. Contraceptive knowledge is available, birth control is encouraged. In the wheat regions where for ages women have been little more than brood mares and not valued as highly, girls married early and gave birth to children regularly. With only ignorance and superstition to guide them the infant death-rate was appalling. With the gradual gathering of the young people of these regions into the collective farms where instruction is given to both girls and boys in sexual hygiene and infant care both the birth-rate and the infant death-rate have fallen tremendously.

Upon becoming pregnant the wife will continue to work, if she is able to do so, but with regular attendance at a pre-natal clinic, until within a month of her confinement. For this month she will remain at home but without any loss of pay. Following her confinement she will remain at home for yet another month, her one duty now being the care of the baby, and again there will be no loss in pay. At the end of the month she will return to work, taking with her her baby which she will leave, if she works in a factory, in the factory nursery. Every three hours during the day she will be given a half-hour off, without loss of pay, when she will go to the nursery, put on a sterilized gown and have a quiet half-hour nursing the baby. At the end of the day she will collect the baby and return home.

" But surely not all women want to work in factories or offices," I insisted to my Russian companion. " Aren't there any ' domestic ' women, as we would call them, in

Russia—women who want to devote themselves to the care of their children and their homes ? "

" Of course there are," replied my companion, the mother of a recently married daughter and an eighteen-year-old boy. " But it is absurd for a woman to devote her entire time to one child or to two or three. If she wants to devote herself to children she can go to the trouble of really learning something about them and then she can take care of a dozen or more. There are many of these women and they are in the nurseries and other places where trained people care for children."

If a conception takes place that is not desired, the woman will go to a hospital for an abortion. It is her right. She is pregnant and does not wish to be. There are no other questions except as to whether this is her first pregnancy. If so, an attempt will be made to persuade her on biological grounds not to have the abortion. If she insists, then it must be done. There is only one thing she may not do—that is, go to an " abortionist ". But of course that is not necessary and there are no " abortionists ", as the abortion can be obtained at the hospital. In former days death from abortion in the sophisticated cities was very high ; to-day it has fallen to almost nothing.

Will the couples we saw starting on their way at the marriage bureau remain " true " to each other ? We must ask this question because the matter seems so important in our world. In Russia the question seems very silly, even impertinent. Who knows ? Who should be concerned about the matter ? It is a matter that concerns only the persons involved. They may settle it between themselves as they choose, but in deciding it the last thought in anybody's mind will be of " sin ".

The woman may not prostitute herself nor the man make a rake of himself, for such conduct on the part of either of them would work an injury to the group. Aside from that all such decisions rest with them.

Instead of an elaborate code of morals difficult to understand and acceptable only on the basis of " authority ", with confusion worse confounded on learning that the code is not followed generally by the " good " people, thus making necessary the learning of a technique for " getting by ", with the conflicts and feelings of guilt that all this carries with it, the code in Russia is very simple, easily understood even at an early age and acceptable. Those things are wrong—because we ourselves have agreed to have it so—that would injure the group. This covers quite simply all essential matters. Matters non-essential except to individuals themselves—often very essential to us in our efforts to regulate other people's lives and somehow make them " moral " according to our way of thinking—are left to the individuals concerned. Dictatorship in Russia carries these things in its train.

And the significance of all this ? It means the accomplishment on a mass scale of what can only be accomplished in America by a long and expensive process of psychoanalysis, individual by individual. It means the taking of neuroticism out of sex, the reducing of sex interest to the biological and legitimate psychological need of the individual. It means making sex a constructive element, a satisfying, vitalizing power rather than a tormentative and destructive agent.

All " sex " is not sexual—far from it. Sex is used to express many more needs than sexual needs. Reduced to biological need, with such psychological need as is inherent in it, sex is not a socially formidable problem. It becomes formidable when it is made to do service for a large variety of non-sexual needs ; when it is made to serve as a vehicle for working out psychological problems of guilt, inferiority, fear.   The strength of the sex " need " is frequently more representative of the psychological than the actual biological need.   Non-sexual needs expressed sexually develop as the result of unwarrantedly over-inhibited emotional needs of children by well-meaning but uninformed guardians of children. With neuroticism out of sex, not only is energy freed for other interests but by-products such as pornography, perversion and the like drop rapidly to a minimum.

Free of undue sexual preoccupation, their biological sexual needs readily satisfied, the Russian youths, both boys and girls, have energy and interest available for other things.   And here we come to another interesting contrast with Italy—the attitude toward work and learning.

Italy has some excellent schools, excellent as measured by the best " progressive " school standards.   These schools, however, are the preoccupation of individuals. They represent no generally accepted social or educational philosophy.   They are the tack-hammer blows of zealous, fine people who exhaust themselves, as we do here, in efforts to make things better.   The State is interested in raising the standards of the schools, not in changing them essentially, but in improving their efficiency.

As is generally known there has been a serious conflict between the State and the Church as to whom belongs the responsibility-privilege of directing the education of the young.   Mussolini, for the moment at least, has been forced to compromise.   The State will take charge of the secular teaching, but hours are set aside during which the priests, who may not discuss politics, may teach religion. The secular teaching of the State (still in considerable part from textbooks prepared for the former Church schools) is set, therefore, against a background of religious teaching. No matter what the State may teach, the Italian youth will be well informed in regard to the Trinity, the Sacraments, the Virgin Birth, the difference between sin and carnal sin and many other things, including the attitude and laws of the Church in regard to morality in general and sexual morality in particular. Education is a much more complicated and bewildering thing for the Italian child than for the Russian.

The interest of the Italian youth in learning is about the same, it would seem, as for the American. For the average youth, one studies because one is expected to— it is just one of those things. There are vocational schools which are popular and in which there is a considerable degree of enthusiasm. In general the education offered is formal, polite and leads to " culture " but with importance still attached to the saving of one's soul. Work— to be sure, one must work to live. However, with a curb put upon an individual's obtaining too much, individual initiative is a bit stifled—no substitute has been provided—so, as little work as possible for as much as possible and preferably a job with a gay uniform where one may boss. This is not to imply that the Italian youth is lazy or indifferent. It is an attempt to express only what would seem to be his attitude toward learning and work in general. He is capable of the same handsome, appealing enthusiasm for Fascism and Mussolini that the Russian youth has for Communism and Lenin —" See what Fascism has done for the people and what it has done for Italy ! Italy is now a world power and nothing can be done without her consent. France—hah ! —she's shaking in her shoes. Let her lift a finger—hah ! "

It is altogether different in Russia. I doubt if there are many children in Russia who know the difference between sin and carnal sin. But they are keen to know about things and apparently they are keen about it because there is something they want to do with what they are learning. Their education is not directed toward " culture "—except perhaps in the finest sense— not even when they are studying so-called " cultural " subjects. Students apply themselves with energy. They are apparently anxious to get through. Not because school is a bore, far from it, but because they are anxious to get at the things they want to do. As a group in a vocational high school for mechanics said in answer to my question, " Why not become engineers ? " : " Many of us would like to. But we are needed right now and we want to get to work. Russia needs mechanics. We can import engineers but we must have mechanics. Some of us will return later and study engineering but now we want to get to work."

And they ask surprising questions. A hundred or more boys and girls of high-school age had gathered about me in the school courtyard towards the end of a noon interval, my camera the point of interest. I had been bombarding them with questions and finally said that I would be glad to try to answer any questions they might wish to ask. I cannot remember them all now, but here are some :

" What do the boys in America (meaning, I suppose, boys of their own age, sixteen and seventeen) think of George Bernard Shaw's statement in regard to Russia ? "

" What do the boys in America think of the conditions in Germany ? " (This was before the advent of Hitler.)

" What do the boys in America think of present international conditions ? "

After more of this (to which I fear I had not given very satisfactory answers, for they finally ended the series with, " Well, what *is* the American boy interested in ? ") they turned upon me as a physician and inquired :

" What is the percentage of industrial accidents in American factories ? "  I did not know.

" What is the rate of tuberculosis in the cotton mills in the southern states ? "  I did not know.

" What is the rate in the northern states ? "  I did not know that, either.

I found an excuse to get away after the next question, " What happens to an American workman who develops tuberculosis ? " for I could answer that with eloquence and take my leave with at least some grace.

The minds of these boys were directed towards organization and conquering things—mountains with their ore, rivers with their power.  I cannot recall even once in Russia hearing " Russia " emphasized.  Communism was emphasized.  " We " always meant " We Communists ", never " We Russians " in the nationalistic sense of Russia as a people apart.  Not only are women human beings but so apparently are Poles, Rumanians and Chinese.  Only the Poles, Rumanians and Chinese don't yet know that ; they still think they are Poles, Rumanians and Chinese.  Poland, Rumania and China, probably now with the new turn in affairs, Japan rather than China, are official enemies, but that is a temporary and more or less technical matter.  They are not really enemies, it is merely that Poland, Rumania and Japan

think they are. Of course as long as these countries
think they are enemies, the danger is real and Communist Russia must be prepared to protect itself. But
these countries, it seems confidently to be believed, will
eventually wake up to the fact that they are after all
human beings, too, rather than just Poles and the like,
and then there will be no trouble.

It seems a curious way to think, perhaps, but there is
considerable evidence that they have reasons for thinking
so. When one considers the bitter antagonisms between
the Czechs, the Slovenes and the Galicians in Czechoslovakia; hatred engendered in the Southern Tyrol as
Italy has tried to incorporate the Austrians into her
state, the former hatreds in Alsace-Lorraine, now against
Germany, now against France, for the same reason, one
sees one side of the picture. As the naïve Russian would
say, this is because these people are not really aware that
they are human beings; they still think they are Slovenes
or Galicians or Austrians or Italians with a history that
goes back for thousands of years. These minorities and
majorities treat each other like some husbands and wives,
each trying to make the other over into something else—
and with about the same success.

In the Union of Socialist Soviet Republics there are
more than one hundred and fifty national and racial
groups. Many of these are composed of large collections
of people settled for years in certain regions. There
is surprisingly little difficulty—and for a reason that
accounts for so many things in Russia. They just turn
things upside down. " Don't ' Russianize' yourself.
Be yourselves. Be human beings with the rest of us,
but in so far as you are different, cultivate that difference.
It is not that we *permit* you to have your own language and

customs and the like : we *urge* you to continue these and
to develop for the good of us all those qualities which are
special to you." And strangely enough it seems to work.
And so the Communist is encouraged to believe that
perhaps some day it will work equally well in Poland and
Rumania and China and Japan—perhaps even in America.

Things have been accomplished in Russia and Italy
that apparently cannot be accomplished elsewhere and
as one observes these things one becomes convinced that
they could not have been accomplished except under
dictatorship. Is dictatorship, therefore, the answer to
present difficulties ? If so, why ? What has gone
wrong with " democracy " ?

The growth of individual freedom during the thousands
of years of man's climb upward has let loose forces that
were not counted upon. Our difficulties are said to be
economic. This is a secondary matter. Our difficulties
are psychological. It is not that we have been over-
spending our money allowance but that we have been
living beyond our psychological means.

Democracy, with its " freedom ", places a premium
on the most primitive, infantile, aggressive impulses of
the individual and heavy penalties upon socialized
impulses. The individual in the church, at the bar, on
the press, in the school, at the bedside, on the hoardings,
whose aggressive impulses are least socialized—that is,
who lives out his personal aggressions directly, like an
infant—and who is, therefore, least able to contribute
to the art of living, no matter what he may contribute
intellectually to the mechanics of living, receives *carte
blanche* in the name of " freedom ". The individual
whose primitive, infantile, aggressive impulses have found
a more sublimated outlet and who is therefore in a

position to contribute not only to the mechanics but to the art of living as well, is destroyed. A system is created in which men, neither " good " men nor " bad " men, but all men, are caught and in which there is adequate outlet for only one part of men's impulses— only the impulses which serve personal ends— " ambition ", " success ", and the like, in terms of individual aggrandizement. Extreme as the statement may seem, the world is under the mastery of primitives ; intelligence, high-sounding titles, dignity do not make the masters less primitive.

Faced with a more immediately critical situation by reason of economic and social collapse in the one instance and threat of collapse in the other, Italy has struck at and Russia has struck down the most aggressive. This could mean one of three things. It could mean merely the exchange of one group of primitive aggressors for another ; or it may mean the provision of a breathing space until other primitives can be trained to take the place of those destroyed—much the same thing in the end ; or could it mean the holding in check of primitive aggression until men can catch up in development and organize a society of individuals whose natural aggressive impulses have not been augmented to a dangerous point by the society in which they have developed and for whose normal aggressive impulses social outlets have been provided ?

Dictatorship alone is not enough. Dictatorship may improve economic conditions, but the psychological benefits of a dictatorship that does no more is about the same as the mental-hygiene value of taking a group of children from the city streets for a picnic in the park. To be of more than temporary value dictatorship must strike not only at immediate aggression but at oncoming aggression, and at the human sources of aggression. The Italian dictatorship deals with immediate aggression ; it redirects oncoming aggression only in part ; it completely ignores the sources of aggression. This is dangerous. The chief outlet for aggression is still other individuals, getting something at the expense of someone else. Collectively it means nationalism of the most ominous sort. The Russian dictatorship deals directly with immediate aggression, but it redirects oncoming aggression away from individuals and to things—the physical world and its forces, the common enemy of all men. Most important of all in its naturalistic attitude towards human relations, particularly in reference to women, mothers and children, it roots up the culture-beds of aggression. In this direction lies energy freed for constructive work and the possibilities of a safe and sound internationalism.

Aggression is not in itself a social ; it is inherent in a human being ; it is the power by which he grows. The significance to others of a bundle of aggression emerging from a uterus will depend upon the handling of that bundle. The bundle goes first into the hands of women. The psychological significance of a dictatorship will depend largely upon what happens to women under it.

The Italian dictatorship is economic and its results are economic. It has no psychological or spiritual values that are significant. Such as there are are secondary, temporary and of little importance, at least for the moment, though there is reason to believe that the square-jawed Mussolini sees beyond what he actually is able to effect. The Russian dictatorship has likewise important economic values, but its greatest and most far-reaching values are psychological and spiritual.

# CHAPTER IV

## OUT FROM CONFUSION

WE are a product of our civilization. We have accepted that civilization and its philosophy in much the same way as we accept aeroplanes or wireless. It has not occurred to us seriously to challenge the principles of that civilization. We have recognized defects in our social organization, and in our various professional ways have striven to correct those defects and to better what we have found. But, whether we have been aware of it or not, at the back of all our efforts have been these principles involving certain concepts of man, and the end towards which we have striven has been the more effective carrying out of these principles in fulfilment of men as conceived.

Our world is unsettled. What has gone wrong? We examine our methods and techniques. We talk about plans. We inquire of the economist, the sociologist, even of the psychologist and the psychiatrist. These cannot help us in any fundamental way. There has been nothing wrong with our methods and techniques. The specialist with his particularized knowledge and technique can be helpful now only as a mechanic. He will discover this and that and direct us how to repair. One cannot be sure that he will be able to put the machine together again, but the best that he can do will be to re-create the machine and cause it to function once more. If he succeeds we may again be doing what we were doing only a few years ago.

But what were we doing ?  We were so busy getting somewhere and somewhere was so near—just round the corner—that it was impossible to see how pathetically inadequate we were even at the moments of our greatest successes.  We were building a better society, on the basis of justice, duty, generosity, charity, derived from brotherly love.  In place of asylums we built hospitals ; for prisons we substituted reformatories and then better reformatories ; for orphanages, homes ; for rigid courts, courts with some semblance of a scientific approach to their problems ; for old types of schools, new types of schools.  We made carefully planned and scientific investigations and demonstrations.  We sought out injustice and unfairness and devised now this law and now that to meet the situation.  How busy and happy we were building a better society—better housing, better working conditions, improved standards of living.  What prodigious effort in time, money and energy !  What rejoicing at our successes !  With what a glow of happiness and satisfaction we reported our progress to our boards and how sincerely did they congratulate us and rejoice with us, for they knew what strength and earnestness had gone into our efforts.  A child-guidance clinic in  Philadelphia !  But  not  only  Philadelphia—Los Angeles, Cleveland, Minneapolis, most extraordinary of all New York City—but also Dallas, New Orleans, Pittsburgh ;  and a booklet full of the names of mental-hygiene clinics started all over the United States.  Could there be any doubt of the success of our years of effort ? But there is a joke in this.

*A* child-guidance clinic in New York City with its one

million five hundred thousand school children. Why *a* clinic in Philadelphia, *a* clinic in Cleveland, *a* clinic in Minneapolis, *a* clinic in Los Angeles and the like ? Does this seem at all strange to you ? It did not seem strange at the time; it was beyond all expectation. It was what we called a " beginning ".

But did it ever occur to you to consider why " beginning " must be made in this way ? What is acknowledged as good for a few hundred children must be equally good for the thousands of children. Why not a dozen or more clinics in New York City ? It is not because there is not need for them. Of course, we understand why—there is not enough money. But really ? We have been given candy and a rubber ball to play with ! And how quickly we have accepted them and what fun we have had bouncing our ball about !

Or did it ever occur to you to consider why there should be *even one* child-guidance clinic in New York City ? Why one anywhere ? Does it seem strange that there should be so many troubled and troublesome children ? However, as you may not all be familiar with child-guidance clinics let us seek our illustrations elsewhere.

Does it seem strange to you that only after mighty effort was it possible to have petrol which, at the time, was a drug on the market, clearly differentiated in the stores from paraffin, then much in use, even though many died horrible deaths from explosion as the result of mistakes ? Does it seem strange to you that only after the most courageous fighting has it become possible to make public announcement of epidemics ? That there must be a *contest* over the matter of pure food and pure drugs ; a *contest*, as yet unwon, over the control of nar-

cotics ? That there must be contests over such matters
as proper housing, child labour, a living wage, work-
men's compensation, unemployment insurance ? One
can understand that much effort might go into the
preparation of an adequate compensation or unemployment insurance law, but once this effort had been
expended, does it seem to you strange that even greater
effort should be needed to have the proposals adopted ?
These are complex problems, you say. Do you really
think that they are fundamentally complex ?

So much are we a part of our own civilization, so permeated are we with its fundamental philosophies, so well
educated are we in its history that it does not seem
strange to us that enormous effort should be necessary in
order to obtain even simple, obvious things. The need
to make effort seems as natural as the air we breathe.
Why must there be effort ? Because others oppose.
But who opposes and why ? Our effort must be expended
in convincing, " educating " influential people who hold
the keys to activity, business men, administrators,
academies of medicine or of this or of that, legislators,
governors. But is it a matter of education ? Do they
oppose on principle ? Almost never ; the desirability,
even necessity, of these things is granted. Is it that
these individuals have other social plans for meeting
these situations and merely are not agreed as to ours ?
No ; they have other plans but they are plans for themselves, far removed from the matter at hand. Our
" education " consists in persuading them that our plan
fits in with their personal plans. In other words, a
problem is not solved readily and easily by reason of its
own simplicity and obviousness, as a child would think.
For reasons a child would not yet understand this has

no bearing; effort must first be expended in overcoming an opposition that is not in any way connected
with the matter. It seems strange and unreasonable
and like a child we would ask, Why?

Organizations of social workers are concerned with
some of the essential activities of social life—health,
living and working conditions, education, child life,
motherhood and the like. Does anyone except the
members of such organizations *really* consider these
things of *first* importance? Social workers are praised,
honoured, patronized; there is lip service from every
" good " citizen, but are there any interests more important to these good citizens? Does even the president
of any organization for social work *really* consider that
the work of that organization is of *primary* social importance? Does any member of the executive board of one
of these organizations, does any contributor? Do you
not know that they do not? These men and women are
" socially minded " people, as good as exist in the land,
but they are also people with poise and judgment. But
—do you yourself consider these things of first importance? Is there nothing more important to you? You
are going somewhere also yourself, aren't you? And
getting on? Or, if you are not, but have sunk yourself
as a sacrifice into the contest, isn't it the same thing
just turned upside down and aren't you a bit neurotic?
Are we then all hypocrites? Not at all; it is not a
question of hypocrisy.

Are the children of New York City and their education more important than Radio City? There is not one
who would deny it, but the denial is idle. The excellences of the one and the defects of the other are true
and representative products of our civilization and repre-

sent what we really think. Is the Harkness Memorial more important than housing? There is not one who would admit it, but the things which the Harkness Memorial represents are considered more important than housing by our best and most " socially minded " people.

There came a time when charity, which had been socially useful in the social period in which it arose, became not only socially inadequate but a socially vicious influence, as it tended to condone and to perpetuate unnecessary human ills. The organizations represented in the National Conference of Social Work, for instance, have been socially useful during the social period through which they have functioned. It is possible, however, that they, too, may become a socially vicious influence as they continue to be an outlet for the " socially minded " with too good judgment. The social worker may come to occupy the place now held by the preacher—the professional tragedy of this generation. Unable to subscribe wholeheartedly to the tenets of his church he began his professional work twenty years ago with some misgivings, perhaps, but with a belief that in the church he could find social usefulness. Disillusionment came quickly in many instances and many conscientious men after suffering much pain left the church for other fields of activity. Others unable to release themselves for one reason or another have remained at their professional duties but without conviction and struggle as best they can with their unhappy lives. The present-day social worker and the organizations he represents may follow the preacher and the church, and social workers may come also to a painful searching of heart as they question whether they are rendering a service or a disservice.

In these difficult times we are told that we should go

to the temple ; that we should get in touch with God.
We do not need to get in touch with " God ". We need
to get in touch with each other. We need to confess our
sins—not our sexual sins ; how ridiculous, how silly, how
unimportant these seem now—but our sins of aggression
against each other. We need to search ourselves and
to discover what is true of ourselves. We do not love
each other. We must admit this. Until we do admit it
there is no hope for us. When frankly we do admit it
we shall, at least, be ready to make a beginning. Pure
selfishness will bring from us a reasonable attitude, even
one of goodwill towards each other, making it possible for
us at least to work together for our joint interests. This
is all that perhaps for the moment we should ask or
expect. We are capable of honesty and goodwill and
perhaps more, but this more can come not through edict,
but through working up from a right beginning. Thrown
out on this ball in space, it would be well for us to take
account of ourselves and our possessions and to organize
ourselves as sensibly as we would were we a shipwrecked
group on a desert island.

As man undertakes to reorganize his life on a realistic
basis he will first consider his own tendency towards
aggression. That man is an aggressive animal does not
come to people with the force of a great revelation, I am
sure. It has been too long known to them as one of
many facts, but when it becomes a reality for them, they
may awake with a start as from a loud noise.

We are aggressive, we must be aggressive. No attempt
should be made to minimize this. It must be openly
acknowledged. Whatever we may wish in the end to
accomplish must be planned for in the light of this fact.
We must be free to be aggressive. The question is how

to manage this aggression, how to turn it to social account. Unacknowledged or acknowledged only in the negative sense of " sin " and unworthiness, lack of goodness, meanness of spirit, selfishness, we are at once divided within ourselves, lose all possibility of integrated, unified activity, must act in any given situation with only a part of ourselves and that part at war with other parts. We must, therefore, act largely blind ; objectivity is impossible.   We can at no point trust our own acts or our own motives.   Where we should be aggressive we find ourselves holding back as in fear.   At other times we know or suspect that we are attempting to rationalize away our aggressions, covering things by fine names.   We catch ourselves in dishonesties and deceitfulness.   We do not know whether we are weak or strong, and if weak how to become strong, or if too " strong " how to check our aggression.   We do not know whether we have a good character or a bad character, nor whether what goodness or badness we find within ourselves is strength or weakness, or how to go about making such change as would seem desirable.   We cannot trust ourselves, we cannot trust others wholeheartedly.   We think we mean well but are not sure.   We think we love others but we can doubt it.   We wish to be loved by others but we cannot trust their love.   Our very best seems sometimes only weakness and not to be trusted, our very worst is frightening.   In either case we do not know what to do about it.

Aggression must be openly acknowledged.   Men must be free to acknowledge their aggressive tendencies without sense of guilt or feeling of inferiority because of lack of goodness of character.   It is not the tendency that is wrong but what the tendency is permitted to do.

You say that this is our present philosophy. Not at all. Our present philosophy condemns and makes guilty the tendency itself ; it condones the act. Not that it intends to, but by creating a sense of guilt over the feeling it succeeds not in changing the force of the tendency but merely its expression, causing that expression to become indirect instead of direct and so confusing us that we find ourselves accepting and condoning aggression under euphemisms. A realistic attitude will neither deny nor condemn the tendency, but it will crush unreservedly any act no matter in what words it is described.

An individual free to acknowledge his aggression is in a position to act with some objectivity. Intellect has at least a chance to come into play and choice tends to become possible. I realize that the matter is not as simple as this, but this will do as a framework for thinking. The question is a complex one and its various psychological and social ramifications cannot be considered here. All that we can do here is to point out the necessity of acknowledging frankly human aggressive tendencies and *to free these tendencies from feelings of guilt.*

Aggression acknowledged, we are faced with the problem of dealing with it. Man must learn to utilize it in a constructive, positive way. He must find means of directing it away from individuals to things. He must find outlets for it through direct and adequate sexual activity, apparently " nature's " outlet, through work and avocation. Further, he must find ways of preventing unnecessary additions to inherent aggression through the frustration of primary aggression. This latter problem, however, will tend to take care of itself as the other problem is solved.

But first men must put down aggression as it exists

to-day. This is the immediate and most important problem. Our social philosophy has permitted aggression to
become riotous. Aggression cannot be organized until
it has first been brought under control. And by aggression one does not mean war in China or Manchuria or
gangster outrages in the large cities. In terms of human
misery they are probably among the less destructive
examples of aggression.

In searching for aggression, let us go not so far afield.
It is the very real but less-obvious aggression with which
we need to concern ourselves. Aggression that bursts
out into the open can be dealt with. Our method of
socialization tends to drive aggression underground
where it continues to exist and to operate in ways far
more socially damaging than when in the open. For
this socially paralysing aggression do not look to the
gangster but to ourselves. Consider, for instance, a
conference of Social Workers : it is representative of
the best in culture and social-mindedness in the country.
Whatever is true of its members will be generally true
of our best. Consider more carefully the president of
any one of these organizations, the chairman of the
executive board, the various members of the board, the
bishop, the university principal, the physician, the
lawyer, consider the prominent contributors. They are
on the whole cultured, educated, soft-spoken, emotionally controlled, not given to open quarrelling, good-
willed, sympathetic, co-operative. But what are their
*real* interests ? Have you worked with them long enough
to note the aggression in them ? In defence of what
and in protection from what do they become " practical ",
begin to quibble, split hairs ?

As between them and the gangster there will be this

difference. The gangster is open and above-board with his aggression. He is out to get all he can, is proud of his prowess and has little sense of guilt. He is not morally confused, he is confused only when he finds that we consider him bad. Our eminent board member, on the other hand, is humiliated by his aggressive tendencies, endeavours to hide them from others and himself, denies them, rationalizes them, dissembles, is disingenuous, intellectually dishonest, shrewd, perhaps sharp, clever, subtle. Having to deal now not only with his aggression but with guilt and fear, he becomes morally confused and ends in being the strange unpredictable person we know him to be with softnesses that shock us and hardnesses that startle us. But, with all, no matter how gentle, he is an aggressive individual as a little observation will abundantly prove. Openly, or more often subtly, but just as surely, he exploits others and under the skin there is no difference between him and the gangster except that his moral confusion sometimes robs him of his courage.

I am not speaking cynically. Again I am not pointing out hypocrisy or a situation that must be considered scandalous. This is all a part of a social order in which the best are caught and cannot extricate themselves. It is to the *system* and the *principles* and *concepts* of that system that one would call attention. One describes only to try to understand. One does not choose the members of organizations for Social Work as illustrations because they are our most outstanding examples. They are representative of the best and finest in citizenship that we have. There are far more obvious examples that each reader can supply for himself. One chooses them because they are representative of our finest and best; we will understand our worst better if we understand our best first.

We, representative of the best citizenship, are exploiters. Behind all we do is exploitation, profit at the expense of others. Our social philosophy encourages it in the name of individual freedom. If man is to take charge of his world, as he has done in Russia, aggression against others, profit at the expense of others, exploitation must come to an end. This would seem to be a primary, fundamental and self-evident proposition. Arguments as to what would happen to " freedom ", " individualism ", " initiative " are without point. These things must take their chances; must take their place as they can. These ideals are the result of men's desires to free themselves from exploitation. They are without value if they lead only to freedom for further exploitation. A freedom which merely means a freedom to exploit under conditions named by the free, is no freedom.

It is not likely that this lesson will be learned easily. We have not to do here with gentle matters that can be dealt with around a conference table, settled by a friendly agreement and the passage of a new law. We have to do with fundamental, even elemental forces, forces that in the beginning probably will yield only to force. And when the time comes when men throw over their false gods and illusions and themselves take charge on a realistic basis, intellect and culture will not be a saving grace. An individual's ability to keep his hands off others is not to be measured by the size of his intellect or the thickness of his culture.

Social schemes that fail to recognize the fundamental situation and that either blindly or openly try merely to rearrange balances of power change nothing. Because of this we can have little faith in measures that are being proposed at the present time. We have begun to hear much of economic planning. Russia, we believe, has brought herself out of chaos through economic planning. After our years of doubt, even scorn and hatred of Russia, we see that such planning is the only sensible way. But it is a serious mistake to think that what Russia has accomplished has been accomplished through economic planning. As so often in America, we are distracted by the big, spectacular thing and miss the chief point. Russia's success is due to the philosophy that lies behind her economic planning. The very thing that Russia scrapped in order to make her planning feasible and meaningful, we retain—so far as any mention of the matter has been made—and hope by a mere social manœuvre to bring success that has come elsewhere only through a complete change in social philosophy. Economic planning as we see it in Russia is indeed a stupendous thing in itself, but it is not the biggest or the most important accomplishment in Russia.

We are undoubtedly capable of making such a plan, but until the men who are to carry out the plan, from the business administrators to the men at lathe or loom, are agreed *not only to the plan*—that would not be so difficult, perhaps—but to *what the plan signifies*, the plan would have less chance than prohibition in New York City. Such planning means either a complete change in social philosophy or an authority sufficiently great to enforce the plan once adopted regardless of what any individual thinks of it. With all our experience we do not seem even yet to have learned that a plan alien to the philosophy of the people upon whom it is inflicted will not work. Our present economic disorganization is not an accident or oversight but a product of our social philosophy. It is as indigenous as a pine tree in Maine. Economic planning is as alien as coconut palms on the shores of Lake Michigan. If we are to have a new plan we must first have a new philosophy. Any new plan must develop naturally from that philosophy. A new plan, which is anything more than a slight shifting of stresses and strains, superimposed upon our old philosophy is an anachronism and must fail.

For this reason one has little confidence in unemployment insurance or any of the other " justice "-bringing schemes. This is just barter and trade. Someone must pay. Those who pay will pay as little as they can, those paid will get as much as they can. The fundamental situation remains exactly where it was before. The only change is that those who have, have a little (very little) less ; those who haven't, have a little (very little) more. And the world goes on until we can think up some other scheme—always a scheme, a plan, some manœuvre, a shifting of this and that on the uppermost surface of things, unaware that the cause of our difficulty lies not in economics and social what-not but in our fundamental concepts regarding men and in our own illusions and the social philosophy we have constructed out of these concepts and illusions.

Is it freedom and right to individuality that we strive for—freedom to live our own individual lives with some degree of satisfaction both for ourselves and others ? If so, we look in the wrong direction for freedom. What we have not yet learned is that there can be no group freedom or individual freedom within the group until the group is composed of spiritually free individuals. This is a matter that can only be touched upon here.

Our bondage is to ourselves. It is first from ourselves that we must free ourselves. An individual's freedom comes first from within, secondly from without. Man out of his own illusions in regard to himself has himself forged the chains that make freedom impossible. Recognizing his aggressive tendencies and fearing them, he has attempted to outlaw them. They remain outlawed but no less effective and controlling. What goes out by the back door comes in through the front door. Full of fears of himself, of guilt, unworthiness, inferiority created within him by the necessity forced upon him to deny and hide what cannot really be hidden, his relations to others become self-conscious. These relations can never be frank and honest. He must dissemble and try to be and to be doing what is expected of him. Eventually he deceives himself, but there is constant danger of exposure either to others or, probably more disturbing, to himself. Most of his energy is consumed in the conflict. His fear drives him to seek security— where he will never find it—outside himself in defensive-offensive group alliances with laws, rules, regulations and eventually armies, and to sanctify in the name of group law and order the very thing he has been fleeing from. The situation is largely artificial and unnecessary. We have created the situation for ourselves by letting men in the name of God tell us what they did not know and devise a scheme of life for us. We can at least now see the pass to which we have come.

But how are we to obtain this spiritual freedom that will make a social freedom possible? Shall we look to the psychiatrists? It has been our method. Were there a thousand able psychiatrists for everyone that now exists we should not touch the situation. With spiritually crippled individuals being turned out by the basketful, what opportunity, on a scale to be socially significant, has an individual, clinical method even under the best of circumstances, and when that work must be done in the atmosphere of the factory that created the condition— what can be said ?   We have a right to be appreciative of such organizations as child-guidance clinics.   They are a partial salvation for individuals but they are not even the beginning of a social salvation.   Individual, clinical methods as a means of social prophylaxis will go with its civilization.   Only a hygiene of society itself will meet the situation.

In the attainment of that hygiene of society there will no doubt be many steps but one of these steps will certainly be to agree to be human beings together ; in the interests of us all, to bring present aggression under control and to keep it under control, not being afraid in our collective interest to use force where necessary ; so to organize our human life together that the mechanics of life can be brought to a minimum, leaving the major portion of our time to live our lives as we see fit, barring only the exploitation of others.   Out of such a life with the realistic philosophy that would motivate it, might come individuals spiritually free and therefore able to be socially free and able also to allow others to be free.

When untroubled by internal conflicts, when no longer individually in the grip of guilts and fears and inferiority —and reacting regardless of the situation to these and to these alone—a group of men sit about a table ; when no man in the group is a challenge to any other man in the group because each man is secure within himself and is psychologically dependent upon no other, men can be honest—they have no reason, conscious or unconscious, to be dishonest ; they can be generous, for they do not need to fear generosity ; they can accept the individuality of others because there would be no reason not to do so.  The individuality, the freedom we seek is possible only among such men.   Such men—and most, perhaps all, men have the potentiality of such men— can never be as long as we maintain a society fostered on illusions that destroy men's potentiality and that deceives itself in thinking that it is working towards goodness when it is working only towards being polite and towards freedom when that freedom is only freedom to exploit.  All that men know about their world they have learned themselves ; " God " has told them nothing. The only thing that " God " has told them that they still believe is about themselves ; let them now investigate that matter.

## CHAPTER V

## CONFUSION LESS CONFOUNDED : A RABBI TAKES UP THE CHALLENGE OF A PSYCHIATRIST

*By* Morris S. Lazaron

" Out from Confusion " is a magnificent protest against the sham, self-delusion and hypocrisy of contemporary life. Dr. Williams's protest is brave, sound and salutary. His evident sincerity made the reading of it a moving experience.

Because I agree so heartily with Dr. Williams's indictment and share his indignation at the cruel wrongs that create human misery I am loath to take issue with him. Yet he has made such summary disposition of matters I deem vital that I cannot keep silent. Certainly if " doctors disagree " in the diagnosis of physical ailments —their own field—I, a mere rabbi, may offer to a learned psychiatrist something of diagnosis and remedy for the social malaise which lies as much in my field as in his.

The chapter begins on the current note of disillusionment. We thought " we were building a better society on the basis of justice, duty, generosity, charity derived from brotherly love ". But we were only making a " beginning ". Every social advance was microscopic and came at the cost of terrific effort. We have had a continual struggle to promote the social good because devotion to the common weal is only a lip-loyalty ; because man is an aggressive animal ; because though he attempts to conceal his aggressiveness beneath an assumption of kindliness he succeeds only in rationalizing his innate selfishness, he does not sublimate it. This dichotomy between what man really is and what he professes to be produces a sense of guilt which expressed itself in compensatory hypocrisy, cruelty, anti-social and repressive laws and institutions.

Dr. Williams declared it is stupid and futile to go to religion. The " preacher " is the " professional tragedy of this generation ". He finds himself torn at every step by the interests of his own inner convictions, his personal needs and the limitations the social order forces upon him. The social worker is in danger of becoming equally futile because he too depends for his livelihood on the very groups which create the problems he is challenged to solve. We cannot find any solution to the problem outside man. God can't help. Man must find within himself the power to curb his aggressiveness and direct it into social channels. This contemplates the acceptance of a new set of principles to govern industry and human relations. And this means open confession that we are not really moved by considerations of justice and humanity ; it means we accept the fact that we are naturally aggressive and selfish. Then having made peace with ourselves by this confession and having thus removed the sense of guilt, we can begin the task of social reconstruction with much greater chance of success.

Dr. Williams resents the slowness of social progress. But when one counts the æons of time it took to make the earth, to develop the animal, to evolve man, why should it be disillusioning to realize that it takes time to civilize and socialize man ? In the natural order pro-

gress is measured by centuries of centuries.  Why should
the cultivation of man's spirit take less time ?

I might say to Dr. Williams that it seems passing
strange too that it takes so long to cure some forms of
mental functional deviation.  As a psychiatrist he might
reply that the malady is the result of long accumulation
of numerous factors ; the disturbance is but the final
result.  But if it takes so long to re-integrate and stabilize
an individual, why is it so strange that it takes time to
bring to fulfilment all the latent nobilities of millions
of human beings in the complex relations of the social,
political and economic order ?

Dr. Williams is on much sounder ground when he asks
why so much effort is required to achieve an obvious
social benefit.  He answers : because the men and women
who support the welfare agencies are torn between two
interests—their loyalty to the organization and their own
personal interest in the preservation of the present social
order, with the latter really dominant.  I put the issue
more sharply.  The social worker is confronted with
problems which have been created by the very men who
support his work.  The system which makes possible
generous gifts creates the poverty which the worker is
called upon to alleviate.  There is no permanent social
usefulness in caring for two hundred and fifty families
this year when next year another hundred will be added
to the list.  The problems are created by defects in the
system.  The duty of our generation is to reconstruct the
system.

Trapped in this dilemma, what is the way out ?  According to Dr. Williams, God can't help.  Religion is
bankrupt ; its leaders pathetic failures.  Social work and
workers are in danger of an equally tragic débâcle,

It would seem that the only logical thing to do would be for us all to resign forthwith as social workers and ministers and join the social revolutionaries. But Dr. Williams proposes nothing so radical as this. He proposes simply that we recognize the devil in man and adjust our ideals and principles accordingly.

But is this idea of his anything so startling or new ? Hasn't Western civilization always reckoned with the devil in man ? For all his denial of religion, is the author not raising the ghost of the old evangelical superstitions ? I am reminded of a familiar quatrain :

> You ask me for something original,
>     I hardly know where to begin,
> For I possess nothing original
>     Excepting original sin.

But Dr. Williams reverts not only to theological patterns—*mirabile dictu*—he actually ascends the pulpit and cries out with the preachers of all time. (This naïve, unconscious reversion is delightful, especially coming from a psychiatrist.)

We need to confess our sins—our sins of aggression against each other. We need to search ourselves and to discover what is true of ourselves. We do not love each other. We must admit this. Until we do admit it there is no hope for us. When frankly we do admit it we shall at least be ready to make a beginning.

Here Dr. Williams, who criticized the " beginnings " of social endeavour, pleads for a *beginning* of his own sort. But is there really any difference between the *beginnings* of child-guidance work in New York or elsewhere and the *beginnings* of a mass recognition that we are all aggressive creatures ? Perhaps these very *beginnings*, child clinics here and there, little oases established after years of arduous labour, result from the silent, persistent influences of those principles of religion, of justice and brotherhood which Dr. Williams minimizes.

However, we should meet the author on his own ground.

In these difficult times we are told that we should get in touch with God. We do not need the temple. We do not need to get in touch with God. We need to get in touch with each other.

This is perfectly plain speaking. Personally I welcome it. It represents the point of view of many people. It is stupid for religionists to throw up their hands in horror and utter " blasphemy " !  Although religion is to me the profoundest experience and the ultimate explanation of reality to which man can attain at present, I am willing to concede that this is but one interpretation of the universe. Other interpretations are held to be true by other people. For me religion represents truth. My desire here is to point out why I believe *religion cannot be ignored in any attempt to solve the problems of social mal-adjustment.*

I admit the tragic position in which religion finds itself to-day. Oftentimes the very men who support church and synagogue are those responsible for the problems that plague us. As I have pointed out from my own pulpit and elsewhere, one of the searching questions that church and synagogue must face to-day is this : are they brave enough to risk the support of rich contributors by challenging the soundness of the entire system which enriches them ?  I maintain that when the record of these terrible years is put down, foremost among the names of those who have preached and practised this doctrine week in, week out will be enlightened men and women in the pews and fearless clergy, Protestant, Catholic and Jewish. This is all perfectly obvious. But it is just as well to state it for the benefit of those who indulge in wholesale condemnation of religion.

But Dr. Williams's point is not whether individual ministers, priests and rabbis have done this; it is rather whether God and church and synagogue are needed. He says No. I say Yes. I say Yes because the dynamic which these men have found, the inspiration of the ancient Hebrew prophets for social justice in the name of the living God, is still the most powerful incentive to stir the will and move the hearts of the masses of men.

Dr. Williams declares that all we need do is to recognize that we do not love one another. Then we shall take the first step out from confusion. I hold that we already recognize this. I suggest further that the mere recognition does not offer sufficient stimulus even for a *beginning*. The majority of men need a greater dynamic than knowledge. I believe we can find that dynamic best in the very churches and synagogues to which Dr. Williams declares that we need not go, or rather to which he says we should not go.

Churches and synagogues represent not themselves but the eternal spirit of justice and human kindness. Many of them are not worthy of the things they symbolize; many seem to care more about the preservation of the institution, its customs and traditions, its credos and theologies, than they do about a juster economy. But at their best they offer stimulus to social responsibility which no amount of knowledge can offer.

Dr. Williams approaches the social problem from the point of view of the psychiatrist. Certain mental maladies are caused by the non-recognition of potent factors that lie beneath the surface of our consciousness. Through the probing of the psychiatrist these influences, ideas, fears and prejudices are brought to the surface ; we recognize how they dominate our conduct. Having revealed them, we are able to release ourselves from them. We substitute something more normal and healing. The method is good in dealing with an individual patient. Whether it will work as a solution of the social problems of our time is questionable. It is excellent to call contemporary society before the bar and indict it of hypocrisy. Society may repent and " hit the sawdust trial ". But I doubt it. To tell a man he is " aggressive " will not cause him to stop being aggressive. He needs another stimulus. I can hear some of the men on our church and charity boards say : " All right, Dr. Williams, I'm aggressive. I know it. But what about it ? To tell society it is hypocritical and self-seeking will not cause society to stop being so. Another, a more vital challenge is necessary."

I'm afraid Dr. Williams attributes a greater measure of developed social conscience than we really have. It is not the *feeling* of guilt or the lack of it that inhibits social advance. I would respectfully suggest that Dr. Williams has got tied up with the terminology, the ideology and the patterns of thinking of the psychiatrist. It is a perfectly understandable mistake. Just as of course he will say of me : " Well, Rabbi, in your plea for religion you are reverting to the patter and patterns of your kind." I'll admit this. But only in part. It is one thing to say to a man : " You've been acting as though you were prompted by the highest of motives whereas in truth you are really a selfish, aggressive and unpleasant fellow. Consequently you are suffering from a feeling of guilt. Recognize the common clay you are and act on it and not only you but everyone else will be happier." That is what Dr. Williams would say. At least so I understand him. But how in the world this will make for a better social order Dr. Williams does not make clear.

On the other hand, say to a man or to society : We are all human beings. We have not only bad tendencies but good tendencies. We are capable not only of selfishness and greed but of goodwill and love. We were created that way. We are all of us caught up in this mysterious experience called life. We are parts of a process which, while at times it seems objective, cruel, ruthless, is at other times intimate, personal, kindly. For every catastrophe I can point to a blessing. The thunderstorm that wrought havoc to crop and habitation cleanses the air, waters the ground and evokes the ministrations of healing and helpfulness for the stricken and forlorn. For every disease the frantic effort to discover cause and cure. For every famine the outstretched hands to feed the hungry. And in your personal life you have known heartache and frustration and despair ; but you have known also work and struggle and achievement, the tenderness of friendship and love, the joy of fulfilment. You do not comprehend it all but faint intimations come to you, whispers that tell you it is " all a part of one stupendous whole " ; that you, one single being, are worthy in the scheme of things. Some intelligence is attempting a glorious adventure with nature and humanity as materials. You are necessary not only to an adequate explanation of the story of life but necessary also to its happy conclusion.

Will you work with that mind and will and love we

call God ?   He expects it of you.   Will you yield to the promptings of the true, the beautiful and the good within you and so in your own life further this mystic process of evolving glory in which we all have a share ?

It seems to me that this second approach, this religious approach obviously offers the stronger and more dynamic stimulus to the will.

But Dr. Williams appears to change the basis of his argument when he declares : " Aggression acknowledged, we are face to face with the problem of dealing with it."   And the method he suggests is : " We must put down aggression as it exists to-day."

This apparently reverses his position.   First he took the ground that to acknowledge aggression and bring it to light would be sufficient.   Now he declares that it must be turned to social account by *putting it down* ; we must not be afraid " to use force where necessary " to put down aggression when that force would be for the common interest.   But what does he mean by force ?   He has decried force from " without ".   He says : " Man's fear drives him to seek security where he will never find it— outside himself in defensive-offensive group alliances with laws, rules, regulations and eventually armies and to sanctify in the name of group law and order the very things he has been fleeing from. . . .   Our bondage is to ourselves . . . an individual's freedom comes first from within, secondly from without. . . ."   But I ask, what is the force from within that must be roused to action and brought to dominate man's life ?

Dr. Williams would say man's better nature.   But I reply, why should one yield to one's better nature ? What indeed is one's better nature ?   What are the values of the " force within " to which one must yield

and what validates those values ? Dr. Williams does
not explain.

That " force within " which Dr. Williams apparently
*ignores or discounts in the first part of his paper but to
which he appeals in the end*, is that mysterious *plus* which
defies the microscope. That is the force which explains
Dr. Williams's own prophetic insight, which uses him as
its efficient instrument.

It is the spirit of man. Also it is man's instinctive
acknowledgment of what is right, his capacity for friendship and consciousness of brotherhood. There are constructive forces just as potent in the creation of a better
social order as these destructive forces to which Dr.
Williams refers. Any analysis of the principles that must
motivate social betterment which ignores them, ignores
at least the half of reality. And this half is the sphere
of religion. Dr. Williams forgets that that force within
has been built up laboriously through the centuries,
through the discipline of experience, the ministrations
of religion which always have held up to man a picture
of what he might be if he would. He forgets that even
beyond all this centuries-old training in religion, there
is the instinctive impulse of man to relate himself to
the universe ; that man came to feel that life is worth
while, goodness is real, sacrifice is necessary, all things
have meaning *because* he related himself to the eternal
spirit. It was just this conscious relation to God that
validated all his experiences. That was the dynamic
that moved man.

When I say God I do not mean an old man with a
flowing beard riding on a cloud ; I do not mean the
Setebos of Caliban. I mean that mind and might, that
will and love, that beauty and glory we sense in the world

round about us and to which in our best moments we feel
related in an intimate and personal way.

I try to do the decent, generous, social thing because
when I do some change takes place within me. I feel
enlargement and exaltation. But I want to do it most
of all because my horizons are widened, because I am
conscious then of a friendliness in the universe, of an
intimacy with seas and stars as well as with my fellow-
men; because my life somehow seems caught up in the
larger process of which I feel myself a worthy and necessary part; because my spirit for the moment seems to
share in the cosmic process; because, in short, I then
joyously recognize my kinship with God and my responsibility to myself and my fellow-men.

Of course I admit these things are not matters of
scientific truth. There is no proof of God save that which
rises out of the inmost being of a man. I know that not
to all is given that poignant sense of His presence. I
know too that religious institutions that have spoken in
His name have in reality all too often crucified His spirit.

It is out of such sentiments, however, of which the institutions of religion are custodians, that the great social
dynamic is born in the masses of men. Without this
dynamic to restrain and humanize it, the social evolution
becomes the social revolution; blood flows, pride of conviction runs riot in the past in the baneful institutions of
Inquisition, pyre and pogrom, and in the present in the
crucifixion of freedom in Russia. Without this dynamic
we build on sand, for there are no values and nothing to
underwrite them if there were. With it we can build
enduringly! Man becomes integrated in his universe.
He will not feel that he struggles alone. He will not
close his eyes to the evil in himself but he will seek to

subdue it ; he will not ignore it, he will sublimate it because he believes in *a power within and without himself* that makes for righteousness.

We have tried law and it has failed. We have tried force and it has failed. Let us now try religion in this largest sense. We have had churches and synagogues and cathedrals ; we have had preachers and rabbis and priests —we've had precious little religion. But in the religious spirit of man is the force that can be tapped to the ever-lasting blessing of society. Not through fear of hell and damnation, nor the arrogant assumption of inviolable authority, not creeds and theologies and ceremonies, but through the frank acceptance of the fact that within us are areas of spiritual power we have not touched, related to that source of inexhaustible power outside us which is God. Man needs to bring this overwhelming force to dominance in his life. Religion is the key which releases it. Once released it will go down into the depths of his being ; it will gird him for usefulness.

We are not only " a product of our civilization ", as Dr. Williams declares. We are the builders of the civilization that is to be. We can diagnose the diseases of society quite readily. Let us not make the fatal mistake of ignoring the most potent factor in the healing of the patient—the religious spirit of man. If we learn to use it properly, this generation will hand down a better world to its children and help to make confusion less confounded.

# CHAPTER VI

## HATE: CONFUSION MORE CONFOUNDED [1]

THE Russian communists renounce religion, the Christian God, and all other Gods recognized at the present time. They are atheists. And yet I am not alone in believing that the Russians have a richer spiritual life to-day than any other group of people on earth. There would seem to be something incongruous in this but there isn't. To renounce religion is more easily said than done. What the Russians have done is to renounce all orthodox Gods and forms of religion and the ideologies that through the ages have been caught up in the various philosophies and systems of Gods. This leaves them without a " God " in any orthodox sense and any religion in a formal sense but not necessarily without religion or indeed without a God. What has developed among them is a Spinozian religion—each a part of a whole. To be sure, it is different from what we have known as " religion ", but it is religion in the sense that it expresses a need deeply felt within man for the security to be found in identifying himself with something larger than himself. It is to this need that the modern preacher refers when he speaks of the religious and spiritual nature of men. Although our modern preachers are inclined to be shocked at the anti-religious attitude of the Russians, one finds it easier to respect the Russians in the position they have taken

[1] The author's reply to Rabbi Lazaron.

than the modern preacher in the position he has taken. The Russian has stripped to what would seem to be bed-rock. The modern preacher has divested himself of all that would seem to make the Christian religion significantly Christian but clings to the names and forms even to personal petition through prayer. A fundamentalist minister praying through a radio is understandable, although his action may seem strange, but a modern minister praying through a radio is simply not understandable. The Russians are consistent and understandable.

The God of Rabbi Lazaron, and so well has he stated the position of religion in general that I believe we can say the God of all modern religionists, excluding the Catholic and Fundamentalist God which is a personal God, is the same as the unrecognized God of the Russians. At this point—the need of men to identify themselves with a larger whole—we stand together, but from this point I fear we diverge until, both seeking the same thing—a satisfactory way of life on this earth—we are in the end far apart. Words, so awkward in the conveying of meaning, or at least so difficult in use, will separate us at first, but it will not alone be words. It will in the end be our different methods of approach to the problem and what we learn from the use of the two methods that will separate us.

This need which we both find in men Rabbi Lazaron would call religious or spiritual. I would question naming it so. It may not matter what things are called and yet it does matter. The words " religious " and " spiritual " have such a long confused history that they are too unclear to be used now in discussing this fundamental need. Using them we would not mean what they imply to

Catholics or to Fundamentalists, nor to people generally ;
we would only mean what they mean to the comparatively few Rabbi Lazarons and Protestant Modernists.
But for the moment let us use the terms and agree that
this need is the basis of religion.  To satisfy this need
of being a part of a whole Rabbi Lazaron finds need to
assume a God, " not an old man with flowing beard riding
on a cloud and not the Setebos of Caliban ", but an
impersonal God.  " I try to do the decent, generous,
social thing because when I do some change takes place
within me, I feel enlargement and exaltation. . . . my life
somehow seems caught up in the large process of which
I feel myself a worthy and necessary part ; . . . my
spirit for the moment seems to share in the cosmic
process ; . . . I then joyously recognize my kinship
with God and my responsibility to myself and my
fellow-men."  " Of course I admit these things are
not matters of scientific truth.  There is no proof of
God save that which rises out of the inmost being of a
man."

Rabbi Lazaron experiences these feelings within himself, finds them satisfying and that they lead him to
acceptable social activity and relationship with his fellow-
men.  He assumes, therefore, that this somehow relates
him to the God he has postulated.  I would not make
these assumptions.  I would rather examine these feelings
to see if I could come to understand the source within
the individual from which they come, why they arise,
why they vary so among men and what their actual
significance may be regardless of any moral, social,
religious, or other implication.  Rabbi Lazaron says that
there can be no scientific proof of God.  Granted, but
that is not saying that there is not scientific data in regard

to man's need to postulate a God and his attitude towards
that God.

Rabbi Lazaron cannot deny me the right to refuse his
assumption and to examine with such scientific tools as
we have the feelings which lead him to generous and
good citizenship and union with God. Not so long ago
rabbis and ministers assumed that bad men were just
bad. Rabbi Lazaron would not do that to-day. He
would welcome, I feel sure, every scientific aid that could
be brought to the better understanding, and through that
understanding possible readjustment, of a delinquent;
but in doing this Rabbi Lazaron exposes his own position.
If science may study a bad man it may also study a good
man; and if it can come to understand a bad man it is
probable that it can come to understand a good man also.
We make no assumptions in regard to a bad man; we
study him. Science makes no assumptions in regard to
a good man. We would not even assume, as Rabbi
Lazaron tends to, that a " good " man, in his sense, is
a good citizen. We would prefer to study the " good "
man's acts as a citizen, as husband, father, associate, and
see what kind of a balance could be struck.

" Any analysis of the principles," says Rabbi Lazaron,
" that must motivate social betterment which ignores
them [the spirit of man, man's instinctive knowledge of
what is right, his capacity for friendship and consciousness of brotherhood] ignores at least the half of reality."
That is true. " And," continues Rabbi Lazaron, " this
half is the sphere of religion." In other words the bad,
or bad impulses, are to be left to science, the good, or
good impulses, to religion. Why?

Rabbi Lazaron and the Christian religion recognize
man as being part good and part bad, as holding both

love and hate, both friendliness and aggression. Rabbi Lazaron and the Christian as well would meet this situation and socialize men by appealing to and arousing the good in men. This can be accomplished, Rabbi Lazaron insists. So have the Christians insisted for more than nineteen hundred years and the Hebrew prophets for longer than that. What reasons are there to believe that it is workable now? Rabbi Lazaron can reply that it has never really been tried. That is true, but isn't that significant? Aside from assumption is there any reason to believe that it is even triable? In the days of the Hebrew prophets or of Jesus Christ there was no way of knowing that such a method was not workable. It was intelligent to try it out, but the method has failed and we are not without knowledge as to why. It is built upon assumption in regard to men and not upon knowledge of men. We are not so lacking in knowledge now as men were then and with our knowledge we are not justified in proceeding on the basis of their assumptions.

If we were to wipe the slate clean and start anew using the same assumptions and the same method we would in the end arrive exactly at the point where we are now. Recognizing the good and bad in man, or, for the moment let us use the terms hate and love, and calling upon man to manifest only love, will mean that he must crush down the hate (it was thought this would mean crush out but we know now that it doesn't). He will not succeed in doing this, as hate *is as much* a part of him as love. The moment he fails a sense of guilt is introduced and once this is introduced the chain of psychological events begins that leads to the kind of people we are to-day and the kind of society we have constructed. It is as though, with two hands, it were morally right to use only the right hand. If such were the case all of us with the best of effort and intention would find ourselves now and then using that left hand. If the feeling of moral obloquy became so great that we bound our left arm to our bodies one knows what would happen in the ache of that arm to be used. Our analogy falls down here as with continued binding the arm would atrophy. Happy were it if hate morally bound would atrophy but it doesn't. It grows and feeds upon itself, seeks devious ways out which are not sufficient, and eventually mounts to the flood point. Then it does flood. It reached the flood stage in 1914 with devastating results. It has passed the flood stage now in many parts of the world and is close to the flood stage in western Europe and America. Swinging incense over these turbulent waters, burning candles at their edge, or offering prayers in the temple or exhorting men to brotherliness will accomplish no more than did the swinging of incense over the unintelligently cultivated Russian wheat-fields to bring forth a greater harvest.

Rabbi Lazaron and the Christians are afraid of hate as they have been afraid of sex which they associated with man's bad qualities. There were reasons for our forefathers to fear hate, there are reasons for us to fear it also when we do not understand it and see only its wild, catastrophic manifestations, but we need to fear it only in this sense. We no longer fear the lightning; we have learned to understand and to harness it and to make it useful. Hate is understandable also and can be harnessed and made useful, but not by the method advocated by Rabbi Lazaron. Prayer did not harness electricity—although the effort was made and is still made to-day—and prayer will not harness hate. Assumption in regard to the nature of electricity did not harness electricity but knowledge attained through investigation, experimentation, and further investigation. Assumption in regard to hate will not harness hate but knowledge derived from investigation, experimentation, and yet more investigation. Hate can be transmuted into energy and this energy used to social ends as any other energy. To recognize hate, as Rabbi Lazaron says he does, but only to cry it down, to make it a bad and guilty thing and to override it with love is not enough.

We must accept man *as a whole* and for what he is and in our planning plan for *the whole*. It will not do to play one part against another. It is true that men are capable of love and goodwill. Love is one of man's fundamental needs and not for any " spiritual " reasons (in the religious sense) but for reasons that are earthy and human and that we can find by studying man himself and disregarding all postulations in regard to God. But man must also (at least at the moment and probably always) hate, and for reasons likewise that are earthy and human and are to be found within him and without any postulations in regard to a Devil or Hell. (Strangely enough, and yet understandably, this statement is understandable and acceptable to most people, while the first statement seems shocking, although God and the Devil have always been parts of a duality. To inquire why it is so much easier to get rid of the Devil than of God would bring us too far afield, but it is a question that anyone who is troubled by the first statement might well ask of himself.)

Socially the problem of hate is more important for us at the moment than the problem of love. Man will work towards love, we may be sure, not because of admonition but even in spite of it and regardless of whether a God is postulated or not. He will work

towards it out of himself and his own needs, but he will
not attain brotherliness in a social sense until other
problems are solved.    There needs to be an outlet for
hate ; so high have the waters risen that there must be
an outlet.    We can take this in a great war if we like, and
take it we will if some other way is not found, but allowing
the flood to break in such wild, destructive fashion is not
intelligent if it can be prevented.    Outlawing war, peace
conferences, disarmament conferences will not prevent
it.    These are instruments of the philosophy Rabbi
Lazaron has been discussing and deal with unrealities.
Any statesman in Europe to-day who took these things
seriously (he must take them politely) would be a fool.
Whatever else these men are they are not fools.    They
are better realists than are pacifists.    Pacifists themselves are not morally or psychologically prepared for the
things they advocate.    They are not morally or psychologically superior to their opponents, it is just their way
of working out their own aggression.    It might be said
that even so they contributed to the social good.    It
would be to the social good if the world were morally and
psychologically prepared for peace, or if there were no
more occasion in the world for force.    Under the circumstances it is but another example of personal emotional
problems blinding individuals to realities, and by the
working out of these personal problems through social
questions forcing others into false positions with attend-
ant subterfuge and deceit.    Brow-beating statesmen into
signing peace and disarmament pacts is about the same
as forcing an alcoholic to sign a pledge without first
having solved the psychological problem within him.    In
a sense it is true that wars are economic and political in
origin but this is only partly and superficially true.    Selfish,

nationalistic, blood-thirsty statesmen who are supposed to make wars are but scapegoats. The making of wars lies within ourselves.

Rabbi Lazaron and people generally are too easily satisfied with the appearance of things ; rather, they are deceived and it has been the " good " in them that has permitted the deception. If people speak gently, are friendly and co-operative, hold back their tempers, and argue reasonably (we are speaking of sincere people, not hypocrites) Rabbi Lazaron tends to assume they are the kind of people they appear to be. To a certain extent they are, but the most that can be said is that the kind of people they appear to be is the kind of people they would *in part* like to be or *in part* have been forced to want to be. But that is not all of the story. Their attitude expresses good intentions but not necessarily intentions that can be backed up. There is no more reason to take them at their face value than to expect the alcoholic who has signed his pledge in good faith to keep that pledge when we know that he cannot keep that pledge, or to expect the person with a broken ankle who says with determination that he will walk to walk when we know that he cannot walk.[1]

[1] There is a little-known essay by Freud on living beyond our psychological means that might well be read at this time. It was published in 1922 when we were in the excitements following the war and did not receive the attention it deserves. It is the first of two essays in a small book entitled *Reflections*, translated by Dr. A. A. Brill and Alfred B. Kuttner. With this I would suggest also the reading of a recent essay by Dr. Ernest Jones of London, " The Concept of a Normal Mind ", to be found in the book *Our Neurotic Age*, edited by Samuel D. Schmalhausen. There are a number of excellent chapters in this book although I do not wish to recommend the book as a whole. This essay by Ernest Jones, however, and the

Religion has been and is an escape from an intolerable situation. So are neuroses and psychoses ; so also are romantic novels, alcohol, drugs, sentimental poetry, and much music. Working on a basis of false assumption in regard to man, although these assumptions at the time were not known to be false, we have constructed a world and a society so difficult and painful that escape from it at times is necessary. We have therefore provided ourselves with escapes and these escapes have saved the sanity and made life tolerable for many of us, probably all of us, some using one, some another but all for the same reason and for the same purpose. The fundamental needs for which religion, in particular (although it is not alone in this respect), has attempted to provide is the need for the security and love man has not found in the world about him. But this is a mere running away from self and the world ; it is not solving self and the world. As a refuge and as an outlet for the need for security, even love, a psychosis is much more adequate so far as the individual is concerned—through a psychosis he can have complete individual satisfaction. Alcohol and narcotic drugs, although not as complete a refuge as a psychosis, are more adequate, while their effect lasts, than religion and not quite so incapacitating socially as a psychosis. Religion is a compromise between actually facing oneself and the world and a psychosis or alcoholic or drug addiction. Religion has been until quite recently, and still is among some, as intoxicating as alcohol. An

essay by Freud are probably the two ablest expositions of certain fundamentals of mental hygiene that have appeared in the English language. One who comprehends fully the contents of these two essays need be little concerned, as regards mental hygiene, that he hasn't a medical degree or a Ph.D. in psychology.

attitude of " moderation " has grown up among modernists just as to-day in reaction against prohibition we in
America tend to approve moderate drinking.  As alcohol
was demonstrably a social evil an attempt was made to
prohibit it, but we now find we must return to it " moder-
ately " for the reason *that men need it*.  Under present
conditions it is *an escape they must have*.  Much music,
poetry, art, literature, are but handmaidens in this
respect of religion, although they have greater possibilities.  Neither an individual nor a society will get
anywhere by attempting to deny what is demonstrably
true and running away, no matter by what name the
process of running away is called—religion, culture, art,
civilization, what you will.

No, we must face about.  It will not be easy.  It
would be easy to say that men have danced and must
now pay the piper, but that is not fair.  It implies a
wilfulness on the part of men ;  that men have done
wrong (constructed badly) knowing better.  Men have
done wrong (constructed badly) not knowing they were
wrong but believing and having reason to believe that
they were right.  It is merely that we can now see that
we were wrong and why.  Our problem is to face it.
After all it is just life.  Life isn't the happy time around
the corner.  Life is as it is and the satisfactions for any
one of us must come from life as we find it.  A bitter
period is apparently ahead of us and, if so, then life for
us will be what can be made from such a period not from
something else.  We can know that it will be a difficult
and bitter period, for while men have probably never
before been confronted with a problem quite so great
there have been somewhat similar, if lesser, periods that
have been difficult and bitter ones.

No, we must face about. The inescapable result of
the philosophy Rabbi Lazaron presents is to force aggression into subterranean channels which work to the surface
eventually in exploitation. It is not possible for it to
end in anything else. Disturbed by what it sees (the
opposite of what it had aimed for), and not knowing,
indeed, that it was unwittingly the chief instrument in
its creation, religion has attempted to hold exploitation
in check, but not understanding how it had created the
situation in the first place it has not known how to apply
a remedy ; the only remedy it has been able to find is
more of the same medicine and this has only increased
the difficulty. Struggling with these difficulties, and in the
name and behest of religion, men have attempted various
forms of social organization from absolute monarchies
to democracies, without success. Men in democracies
have attempted to diagnose the difficulty as " bad men in
important places " and to offer as a corrective " good
men in important places ", without success (*The Auto-
biography* of Lincoln Steffens answers this). Men have
tried reform, meaning thereby more adequate checks
against exploitation, without success (John Chamberlain's
*Farewell to Reform* gives a record of this). Now in
democracies men attempt to grapple more definitely with
exploitation and propose measures known as socialistic
that to some are so revolutionary as to create panic
within them and yet which are totally inadequate because
they leave still the principal of exploitation—a nicer
exploitation to be sure, a more " equitable " exploitation, but nevertheless exploitation. This is but tempor-
izing with the Devil. The denominator that is common
to all of these activities and which is fatal for them is the
assumption that man is good and bad and that he can be

socialized by encouraging the good and holding in check the bad.

No, this philosophy and all its derivatives in the form of present-day religion and social organization must be scrapped, not temporized with but scrapped. The question is, how? The answer is not difficult but the way is very difficult and there will be much hesitation before men take the way, although they will do so eventually.

It isn't, however, as though we had a real choice—shall this transition be made peacefully or by force? It will be by force eventually. The bad, the hate, that good men thought they were exterminating, has not been exterminated. It is all there and magnified by the very process that was used in attempting to exterminate it. We are faced with *a situation* and we are left without choice. More of the same treatment will only make things worse. The only choice left to us is whether we shall recognize the situation, attempt to understand it, and understanding, attempt to control it, or refusing to recognize it, or completely misunderstanding it, let things go their own blind way. This can only mean wild, destructive wars on a nationalistic basis that will eventually involve us all. Here men will find an outlet for their hate but with nothing in the end accomplished.

Love for the moment is not the important thing. Hate is the important thing. *We must be permitted to hate.* Realizing that we are not starting *de novo* and cannot have things as we wish but must take things as we find them and deal with situations that exist, there must be an outlet for hate. Can there be any other outlet than just blind war—can we hate with discrimination? We could doubt this were it not that actual evidence of its possibility is before us.

One evening, never to be forgotten, on my first trip to Russia I sat in a policeman's club and listened to a group of youths, sons and daughters of the policemen belonging to the club, singing patriotic songs. One song had to do with the trouble the Russians had recently had with the Chinese. Verse after verse told of the wicked actions of the Chinese as they rushed over the border and murdered fine Red soldiers, of how bravely the Red soldiers fought and died and how in the end they put the terrible Chinese to flight. But it was the last verse or two that attracted my attention and made an indelible impression. In these verses, which the youngsters sang as lustily as the others, they went on to explain that these Chinese soldiers who had crossed the border were not in themselves bad men but that they had been misled, that they, the singers, did not hate these Chinese, although under the circumstances they had to be killed, that they did not hate the Chinese people, that the Chinese people were a fine, intelligent race of men, that they would gladly be brothers with the Chinese and work together with them, but that they did hate certain Chinese who, in China, deceived, misled, and exploited their own people. For these Chinese they had an undying hatred.

It is not a difficult thought to understand. It is not particularly a new thought and yet on that evening it seemed to take new meaning. It was no longer just a theory or a philosophy or a wish ; it had become an actuality. We Christians say these things weakly out of one side of our mouths and leave it to the Russian atheists to speak out boldly our " Christian principles " and to act upon them. These youngsters did discriminate ; they actually hated what to all is hateable. It represented an internationalism that was intelligent. That this could be a common feeling seemed too impossible to be true so that one felt the necessity of finding out. Inquiry among students, whenever the opportunity arose, in regard to their attitude towards the enemies of Russia confirmed that the point of view was not confined to a song. Immediately one contrasted this with experiences elsewhere.

Ask a German, almost any German, in regard to Poland and he will reply that *the Poles* are a bad, aggressive, vicious people, who have stolen a large part of their territory and from whom they must eventually wrest this territory. Ask a Pole in regard to the Germans and he will reply that *the Germans* are a selfish, aggressive people who years ago invaded their territory and stole their land, who are as aggressive and ugly now as then and against whom they must be prepared to protect themselves. The Rumanians say the same of the *Bulgarians*, the Bulgarians feel they have a right to hate *the Jugoslavians*, and the Jugoslavians *the Italians*. The Croatians hate *the Serbs* in their own country, the Czechoslovakians hate *the Germans* and the Czechs within Czechoslovakia hate *the Slovenes* in the same country and vice versa. Italians hate *the French* and the French scarcely conceal their hatred for *the Italians*. Only a short time ago we were preparing to hate *the Japanese*. With the exception of Japan these are all Christian countries and not " modernly " Christian but thorough Catholic Christian.

A Russian youth (atheist) says, " The Poles," (or perhaps it is the Rumanians you ask him about) " are our enemies. They dislike and are afraid of us and may attack us. We must be prepared against them. We shall have to kill their soldiers if they come, but it is a great pity. These Rumanians and Polish soldiers are all right, but they have been misled and deceived in regard to us. If we had an opportunity, if a soldier were a prisoner, we could convince him that we are all right, too, and are not his enemy. We do not hate the Poles or the Rumanians, they are good people—but we do hate *those individuals* in Poland and in Rumania who exploit the other Poles and Rumanians and deceive them in regard to us. These we would gladly see exterminated."

As we have no choice between a peaceful world and a warring world, which attitude is the more intelligent ? As there must be an outlet for hate, which outlet is better, blind, general, nationalistic wars, or wars, indeed civil wars, that may have some semblance of meaning ? Civil wars to end civil wars or just another war to end something or other as it has been in the past ? That will depend upon what follows. This can be a rationalization just as all of our war slogans before have been rationalizations ; but before war did not deal with realities and war had to be rationalized. To-day we are not under the same necessity to rationalize force (and we must be careful that we do not rationalize peace). At any rate the choice is whether men will choose to fight each other as national groups or whether men will see soon enough that their difficulties are not *the* Germans, *the* French, *the* Italians, *the* Japanese, *the* Americans, *the* Peruvians, *the* Bolivians, *the* Colombians, but *a system*—and not only an economic system but a philosophical system ; the one is but the product of the other—and men within their own borders representing that system, and whether, to protect this system, they will align themselves with these men within their own borders in order to attack similar men aligned with similar men in other borders protecting a similar system, or whether refusing to do this, no matter what the slogan, each attempts to take care of what, common to all, is wrong within its own borders—the system and the men representing that system.

So far as the present economic situation in America is concerned there is no solution of this problem until the problems of Europe are settled and under the present social organization, the result of a social philosophy derived directly from a religious philosophy, there is no solution to these problems. Shuffle the map of Europe as you will and there is no possible arrangement that could be satisfactory to all. The Versailles Treaty may have been unfair in its arrangement of territory, but make any other arrangement and it will only be unfair to someone else. The only possible method for any country in Europe to-day is protection, the building up of patriotic fires in the hearts of youth and the fires of hate against other nationals. There can be no solution of European problems until there is an end of political and economic nationalism. There can be no end to nationalism until there is an end to exploitation. Exploitation lies at the base of all these difficulties and so long as our social system remains organized on the principle of exploitation (no matter by what fine names it may be called) pacifists and treaty-makers will not change the relationship between nations in any fundamental sense. The Reverend John Haynes Holmes, a modern and liberal minister who, like Rabbi Lazaron, one can respect although one holds him to be wrong, says (*The New York Times*, February 27, 1933, report of sermon), that President Roosevelt, the Pope and the Mikado could put an end to war by joint action. They can do no more than sit

on a hot lid and they will keep that lid down just so long
as they can sit.   It is not the lid we need be concerned
about but the fires underneath that lid and sitting on the
lid will not put out the fire.

As I have said pacifists are not themselves morally or
psychologically prepared for the things they advocate.
They are not morally or psychologically superior to their
opponents.   They are essentially like them except that
superficially they use different methods.   Scratch any
pacifist and you will see.   His campaigns are just his way
of working out an aggression ;  but even so, it may be
inquired, why not a better way ?—certainly better than
hate worked out through war or even hate worked out
through civil war.   While this superficially appears so,
the answer must be no, first, because he deals with unrealities and cannot therefore succeed, and second,
because he deceives himself and the world in general as
to what he is doing and why and thereby perpetuates a
philosophy that is at the heart of our difficulties—that
men *must* love each other, that brotherhood can be
obtained by demanding it, and through punishing those
who are unbrotherly.   We must get home to ourselves that
the making of wars, dishonesty, deception, and unbrother-
liness lies within us.   In the last analysis wars are not
made by wicked statesmen, by infuriated nationalists, by
"capitalists", by economic conditions, by munition makers,
and the like.   These are straws that break the camel's back
or agents, but agents only, of ourselves.   The agents are
merely realists who take advantage (and profit) of our
readiness.   As long as, with our comparatively simple
problems to discuss and solve, we cannot have peace and
brotherly love in families, in church organizations, in
charitable organizations, in peace committees, university

faculties, representing the flower of trained intellect, why do we think there can be peace between nations ? For the causes of war why do we look further than ourselves ? The president of an international peace society is no better than we, a Japanese statesman is no worse than we. We are both and both are possible because of us and for no other reason. There is a Japanese statesman in the president of the peace society and a president of a peace society in the Japanese statesman. *The duality is us.* No Jesus Christ can bring us higher than our capacities and no Devil can plunge us lower. The capacity to love and the need of man to love and be loved is a reality ; the capacity within man to hate is likewise a reality. The duality is a reality and in any plan it is this *duality* that must be taken into consideration. A timid, weak, unhappy recognition of this is not enough. Recognizing the hate side of man with chagrin and humiliation, as a poor relation, with the plan only of keeping him in the back-ground and out of sight, is not enough. Love and hate are equal partners, in fact to-day they are unequal partners, because of our " poor relation " treatment. The only " civilized " provision we have made for him is to let him work himself out on criminals, foreigners, Jews, Negroes, " Reds ", Communists, "radicals ", bull-fights, cock-fights, prize-fights, wrestling-matches, criminal romances, and the like and, of course, the right to exploit others. The first are not enough and the latter brings destruction.

We must hate. We may start by hating " systems " or a system, but let us not deceive ourselves. We shall end by hating individuals and these individuals will not be " bad " men in any ordinary sense. They do not consider themselves " bad " and we cannot. They are merely men who, working mostly within the range of the moral and legal " rights " we have given them, have come to positions of eminence and power and eventually to represent the system that is condemned. Although it is *a system* that is indicted it will be *men* who will be attacked, or rather who will attack (consider Fascist Italy, present-day Germany), for these men conscious of their rights, sure of their moral integrity, mystified by the bitter criticism they find mounting about them, will not wait to be attacked but will attack their accusers. Then the issue is joined.

What comes out of this conflict will depend upon whether there is a clear notion on the part of those who attack the present system as to what another system might be. Fortunately we are not left entirely in the dark nor is it necessary to discuss either psychological or social possibilities alone on theoretical grounds. Because we have greater knowledge of men than formerly we should be able to plan better. We shall first disregard all former assumptions and act upon what knowledge we have. Man requires security and love ; he also is capable of hate. Provision must be made for both. Not finding security and love in the world about him, man was forced to postulate a God to whom he could flee, and in whom and in the religion built around Him he could find these things. Refusing to flee we shall face the world that seemed so formidable and attempt to solve the problem of its formidableness. We will use the same methods here as have been used successfully in solving the hard physical problems of the world.

We have to do with two situations, an immediate and a future. Provision must first be made for the excessive amount of hate now existing. We shall admit that men have a right to hate and to destroy that which oppresses them. (Any effort to find another way, to solve the problem by " reasoning " one with another comes to this —surely, when through reasoning those who exploit agree to cease exploiting and to permit men to live co-operatively together. It is not the " radical " who first applies force. The " radical " attempts to reason. Eventually his " reasoning " is met by force, then " reasoning " stops—consider present-day Germany, Austria, Fascist Italy, old Russia.)

Freed from exploitation, man's spirit is freed. He can, on the one hand, withdraw his aggression from men and direct it at things ; he can, on the other, turn with greater confidence to men for love, friendliness and brotherhood. Postulating no God, but in a union with his fellow-men, in an identification of himself with the group in a common effort against the physical world, their common " enemy ", men will find the security they require. Does this require a change in " human nature " ? No, it utilizes human nature in all its aspects. It violates only that view of " human nature " that insists that it is " human nature " to exploit others, that only through permission to exploit can individual initiative be attained—which is a burlesque of human nature in that it calls " natural " a condition that men have artificially created.

A social order developed on the basis of men's needs tends to remove those factors that augment the development of aggression within individuals, so that in the developing child aggression may be kept to the minimum (useful and necessary as energy) rather than raised to the maximum, when it becomes socially destructive. It is at this point that we can begin to talk of " sublimation ", not at the point Rabbi Lazaron discusses it. In the end, each identified with a larger whole, we may find ourselves with a Spinozian religion. But what of that ? It is not a word one fears, but what that word stands for.

Rabbi Lazaron chides me with being impatient. I am not impatient. To have watched the world evolve and to have evolved with it at the rate we were evolving in 1913 would have been suitable to my personal temperament, but we are not permitted to do so. A great deal has happened since 1913. It is events that are impatient, not I. Much as we might prefer it, we are not permitted to sit quietly and contemplate the evolving world as in 1913, and no one of us and no group of us will control the pace of events. The best we can do is to give up the mood of 1913 and try to understand what in its revolutionary way is going on about us.

# CHAPTER VII

## YOUTH AND THE PRESENT-DAY WORLD

In the years immediately following the World War there was considerable talk of a " lost generation ". This generation was composed of young men who had been in active service during the war, who had returned to their homes uninjured, but who, because of the experiences through which they had passed, found it impossible to pick up their lives and to find meaning and significance again in living.

It is possible that another generation is about to be lost, and in as tragic a fashion. Throughout Europe are hundreds of thousands of adolescents and young adults wondering what to do with themselves and waiting for —they have no idea. These youths have finished their school preparation and are ready and eager, or were ready and eager, to apply themselves usefully. Many thousands left the high schools and the trade schools four years ago well prepared for useful and necessary pursuits but have not earned since that time one week's regular wage at regular employment. Whatever they have earned, and it has only been little, and here and there, has been on odd pick-up jobs that had no relation to their training. Other thousands have been waiting for three years ; still others for two years ; others for a year ; and others have recently left school to add to the accumulation of those who are trained and waiting.

Some more fortunately placed have utilized their time in further formal study and are ready to be lawyers, doctors, teachers, ministers, scientists, but are now adding themselves merely to those who completed their training in these professions four and five years ago but who are not yet able to maintain themselves in their professions, and if maintaining themselves at all are likely to be doing it at something quite apart from their professional training. This is not true of one country alone, but is more or less true of every country in Europe, with one very great exception ; it is particularly true of Germany, Austria, Hungary, Jugoslavia, Bulgaria, Rumania, and the other Balkan states.

During the past two years we have seen this situation developing in the United States. The American situation has been considered serious, but it has been nothing as compared with the situation abroad. It would be comparable only if every possible personal resource of millions of families was absolutely gone, and there remained for some a public dole of a shilling or two a day and for others nothing at all. The result in terms of human beings, as observed abroad, ranges from despair that ends in chronic, neurotic illness or suicide, or desperation and revolt which ends in crime, preoccupation with sex, usually abnormal in character, either for gain or as escape from the monotony and misery of living, or the combination of both,[1] to banding together for sport in order to maintain physical health and to get such pleasure as can be got from sun, wind and water,

[1] Well-informed observers in Berlin state that ninety per cent, perhaps more, of the youths who are living homosexual lives there are not homosexual but have adopted homosexual living as a means of living at all.

which costs nothing, to banding themselves together in social-political organizations to march and shout and fight similar youths in opposed organizations and all to shake their fists at the national neighbours. The less thoughtful who identify themselves with these organizations accept the doctrines of the organizations which rationalize for them their difficulties, and are buoyant and full of enthusiasm ; but there are many members of these organizations, and many more who remain outside, who do not accept completely or do not accept at all these rationalizations and, with nothing with which to identify themselves, become bitter and cynical or just bewildered.

This condition of enforced idleness, of hunger, misery, despair, illness, rebellion, whether here or in Europe, is due we say to the " depression ". That is true. But there is something here that was observable even before the so-called depression. It is worth while calling attention to it for it is a question whether the problems of the depression can themselves be solved with any permanency and the world be placed upon a going basis until this problem is solved.[1]

In the " good years " immediately preceding 1929 there was coming into psychiatric practice a type of case that now seems full of significance. Parents were increasingly complaining of the lack of ambition of their children, often it was of children in the high school, still more

[1] To understand what has happened to the youth of Germany and why, see *Wir Jugend ! Ein Bekenntnisbuch der deutschen Nachtkriegsgeneration*, by Kurt Massmann. Berlin : Verlag, E. S. Mittler u Sohn, 1933. When a representative of the youth of America can write a *Wir Jugend !* trouble of the present German kind will lie not far ahead. This is an extraordinary revealing book. It should be translated, not as a Fascist propaganda document, but because of its social and psychological significance.

often of youths at the universities. The complaint was usually that the youth had no interest in his work at the university, seemed to have no interest in anything whatsoever, except possibly in having a good time, although not always even this, could not make up his mind what he wanted to " be ", had no powers of application or concentration, dodged responsibilities, even responsibilities he had assumed himself, balked at any scholastic task that required any special effort. Even in some instances where the boy had decided that he wished to become a physician or an engineer, he failed to apply himself to the task of mastering the basic sciences or the required mathematics, gave up his plans and now did not know what he wanted to do. The psychiatrist was asked to give this boy some ambition and to make him see how important it was that he complete successfully his work at the university. All usual pleas had been made—to the boy's own pride, the family pride, duty, responsibility, sportsmanship, necessity. The psychiatrist was supposed to have some other means of getting this boy to work. An interview with the parents not infrequently ended with the statement, " Since he has been at college he has got into a bad crowd. There is nothing vicious about the crowd ; they are just time wasters. They spend their time talking, talking and neglecting their work. They are bad companions for him."

The boy or girl failing at school or university is certainly not a new problem. Boys and girls have long failed at the university for many reasons well known to the psychiatrist. That a boy (or girl) of university age should not yet have found a field of work that interests him, is neither surprising nor new. None of the symptoms mentioned by the parents are surprising or new.

The significant thing is that upon examination of the student one did not find, back in the good years, the usual causes for these symptoms. And often one did not even find the symptoms. There was no real lack of ambition, no lack of interest, no wish to dodge responsibilities, but an earnest and bewildered boy or girl who had been stopped, not by the difficulties of a science or mathematics course, but by questions that had arisen within them, questions to which they sought answers without success and yet questions which, unanswered, robbed them of such ambition as they may have had on entrance to the university. What is it all about ? Why am I here ? To what end am I studying a foreign language—to none so far as I am personally concerned, but to what end so far as the university authorities are concerned ? To what end am I studying any particular course in my schedule ? Some of them are somewhat interesting. Most of them are a terrible bore. At the end of so many more terms I shall have completed a university education. To what purpose—that of being an educated gentleman ? But what is an educated gentleman ? And to what purpose does one become an educated gentleman ? Is the purpose in studying these subjects that I may live more successfully ? But successfully for whom or for what or in what sense ? My father went to a university. I know many college people, many who were quite successful in college, but what has all this had to do with the ways they are living now ? Mother has not read a French book since she left school, although recently she has begun to take two lessons a week in conversational French from a French lady who goes from house to house. Why is she doing this ? Is it anything more than a way of killing time because she is bored ?

Her education does not seem to have kept her from becoming bored in early middle age like anyone else. Another friend's mother has taken up art, another singing, and still another attends every lecture on " psychology " that she sees announced and reads the books as fast as they come out. Why should these women at the prime of their lives be so bored that they must find something with which to kill time ? If their education filled them with such a thirst for knowledge of French, or art, or music, or psychology, why has it been these twenty years in manifesting itself ? Taking care of my brother, my sister and me may have consumed time and energy, but not so much as all that. A richer life ? Does only a university graduate live a rich life or even a richer life ? Is the basis of a rich life two years of French or German, a course or two in mathematics, preliminary courses in one or two sciences, a course or two in history, a survey of English literature, perhaps an extra course in Shakespeare or Elizabethan literature, a course in sociology, a course in psychology that tells how light is refracted through the lens of the eye, at what rate a muscle fatigues, and the difference between a hot and cold nerve ending ? If these things are vital and make for richness of living, why have so many university graduates I know dropped them like hot cakes and now confine their reading to *The Saturday Evening Post*, detective stories and a few current novels that get talked about, their philosophy to popular " outlines ", their sociology and economics to weekly periodicals and political addresses over the radio. A broad-minded outlook on life ? But the president of the university is not a broad-minded man. Help in business ? For what purpose business ? One must make a living no doubt, but beyond that, what ? What

are business men doing ?   What are they doing it for ?
What do they want ?   Where are they trying to get ?
Why do they want to get there ?   As preparation for a
profession ?   I once thought I wanted to be an engineer,
but what is the purpose of being an engineer ?   One
builds bridges or one builds buildings, but why ?   If
somebody wants a building built or if somebody wants a
bridge built, one builds them.   Thereby one makes a
living, but why should the building or bridge be built,
except that somebody wants them and can pay for them ?
Should they be built ?   What essential purpose have they ?
Perhaps there are enough buildings where this one is to
be located or perhaps the bridge will interfere with something else.   What is the purpose that lies behind all this ?
What have I done, after I have done this ?   Apart from
myself whom have I served ?   In my own interest have I
probably performed a disservice ?   There doesn't seem to
be any particular sense to being an engineer any more
than a business man.   I have thought of medicine and I
have thought of the law.   I know some doctors and I
know some lawyers whom I personally respect, but as near
as I can see there is a lot of sanctimonious talk about
both of these professions.   There are no doubt fine men
in both professions, but I don't see that they have much
chance.   In the last analysis, it is a scramble to get the
bills paid at the end of the month.   The doctor may not,
like the business man, leave his charity at the end of his
life to an orphan asylum, but may distribute it along the
way ; but in addition to this charity he must develop a
" good " practice, or he will become an object of charity
himself.   No, I can't see that it has any sense.   If my life
is to be lived for myself alone—and I do not see that
anyone else's life is lived for any other purpose, or, at

least, that it eventuates in anything else, no matter how
sanctimoniously they talk or others talk about them—if
it is to be for myself alone, if it is to be rich and happy,
I do not see that I need to parade through a set of university courses. The parade does not seem to lead to
anything that has any sense to it, but only to a mob that
keeps milling about without any notion of what it is doing
or why, or where it is trying to get.   I do not know what
to do or where to go.   All I can see for the moment is
what to keep out of.

There have long been answers to the questions the
boy has raised.   From one source or another he has heard
them all without being impressed.   The boy indeed does
not represent a psychiatric problem in the sense of a
problem produced by conflict within the boy which he
projects upon his environment.   Such elements of this
kind as there may be are inconsequential as compared to
the reality situation in which he finds himself.   The father
was right.   The boy has been in bad company, but not
just for the year he has been in college, but for the past
eighteen or nineteen years.   The boy's bad companions
have been his parents and the lives they have lived.   The
boy has indicated his view of the mother's life.   What has
been the father's life ?

He has got up in time to have a hurried breakfast
and to catch the seven-fifteen train.   He has worked
busily all morning at his office.   At luncheon he has had
an important business conference or has rushed out for
a hurried bite.   He has worked hard all afternoon and
almost missed the five-thirty train home because of some
irritating details that came up at the last moment.   He
has arrived home dog-tired, the business of the day still
spinning in his head.   This schedule the family knows

well for he has often told about it. At dinner he is
probably silent or irritable. He is mostly too tired to
accept invitations to go out to dine or to have guests come
in. Discussion of either—at the hurried breakfast,
perhaps—is likely to start the day off badly for everyone.
Dinner over, he sinks into a chair, thumbs through two
or three magazines, finds nothing to interest him, is
annoyed by what others are doing, spins the dial of the
radio, finds nothing to listen to, expresses annoyance at
what others are doing now, and finally goes off to bed,
to get up in the morning in time to catch the seven-
fifteen train in order to do it all over again.

The only pleasure the father seems to have is his game
of golf on Saturday or Sunday ; and if it rains on these
days, the bottom drops out of the world for the whole
family. This is one of the things that puzzles the boy.
He can well believe that at one time his father enjoyed
his work, but he is under no delusion that his father
enjoys it now. He does it because he has to, because he
can't stop, because he doesn't dare stop. And with all
his work he does not seem to get anywhere. With the
years, the tensions, the anxieties, and the worries seem
to increase rather than to decrease. Although he makes
a good deal of money, there never seems to be enough
money. There is always something he is concerned
about. Once, in addition to the regular bills (always too
large and always a source of trouble) there were the pay-
ments on the house. Now it is the upkeep on the house
and taxes, various kinds of insurance, and school fees.
With much coming in and with as much or more going
out, the family is well and constantly aware of the father's
anxieties. Money, money, always money ! It is a
theme that has sounded through the home since his earliest

memories and with such reverberation as to drown out almost all other themes.

He has heard that his father was something of a " radical " at his university and known as an idealistic and high-minded youth.   There are traces of this to be seen yet, but the boy knows that, no matter with what idealism the father twenty-five years ago entered upon his work, he works now because he must and for money with which to meet the bills at the end of the month and the other obligations that seem to mount and mount without end ;  and so far as the boy can see this is what he is going to continue to do until he is sixty or sixty-five when he will suddenly drop off and that will be the end— an end, so far as the boy can see, before there was a beginning.   What has it all been about?   Who was served ?   What was served ?   With all this effort, what ?

The boy can see that the father has attempted to build about himself things that would be a joy and satisfaction to him—a home, a wife, and some children.   But the boy cannot see that these have been a joy or satisfaction. He has never had time and has always been too tired to enjoy them or to get satisfaction from them.   There have been moments to be sure, but they have been brief, and as the years have gone on the boy has become fully aware that, loyal though the father has tried to remain, the family has become a burden.   Tension has increased between the father and mother until any satisfaction there may once have been is gone.   Misunderstandings have increased with the children until they are not only no longer a satisfaction but an added source of worry and anxiety.

And that this situation is not peculiar to his own home the boy is well aware.   The situation is the same in the

homes of his companions, both boy and girl.  In fact, he
realizes that in some respects he is fortunate, for in the
homes of many of his companions the situation has got
to a much worse pass.  And all these fathers, working,
working, catching the seven-fifteen train in the morning,
and the five-thirty back in the afternoon ;  and all these
mothers, restless and dissatisfied, dashing out to play
bridge, or having a lesson in French, or one in art, or
one in dancing, and all of them wanting to know about
" psychology ".  What is it all about and to what purpose, and is it for this that one prepares oneself at the
university ?

The boy I have been quoting is a real boy, although as
I have presented him here he is a composite of many
boys seen not just recently but back in the " good " years,
yet the full significance of his difficulties have become
apparent only now.  Some of these boys and girls are able
quite well to put their ideas into words.  Others are less
able to express what they feel and think and express it
only in part.  Still others are just bewildered.  But what
underlay all these things, as one sees it now, and what I
believe is more important now for the youth of the
country generally than the immediate difficulties due to
the " depression ", and accountable not only for the
symptomatic behaviour mentioned here, but for the deep
cynicism that seems to pervade both the universities and
the schools, is that youth, full of energy and idealism,
finds no purpose (except as he may have a personal
ambition which represents the working out of a conflict
within him) to which he can tie, and lacks, therefore,
motivating power.  He finds no purposes to take over
from us.  Insofar as he finds a purpose in us at all, he
finds it without sense.  The very lives of his parents are

evidence of the senselessness of their purposes.   He is in
a difficult situation and so is anyone else who attempts
to talk with him.

His grandfather, or at least his great-grandfather, had
God.   There was purpose in his life, for whatever else
he might do his chief aim was to serve God and to make
himself worthy of the reward God had prepared for him.
This means less than nothing to present-day youth.   His
father, as a youth, had the idea of Service.   His purpose
was " to make the world better because he had lived in
it ".   Whatever else he might do, his chief purpose was
to act in the common good.   He might not have been one
of John R. Mott's Student Volunteers whose slogan was
" The salvation of the world in this generation "—how
strange this sounds now—but whether so specifically
devoted to the salvation of the world or not, he could as
lawyer, physician, even business man, serve the common
good, and this was the power that motivated him as he
learned his German grammar or ploughed through difficult courses in science or mathematics.   But this means
nothing to the present-day youth, at least in these terms.
He is too well aware of what his father's generation of
" service " has meant.   It is too evident who collected on
this service, and that it is as inept and unreal a social
method as " the getting ready to meet God " method of
his grandfather.   Instead of leading to a better social life,
it has led directly to greater social confusion.   Discard-
ing these the boy finds nothing else.

This is true throughout the western world.   It is serious
enough that hundreds of thousands of youths have no
jobs, but that is not half so serious as that millions of
youths have no purpose.   In Europe there is one exception and two partial exceptions—Russia, Italy, and Ger-

many.  In Russia youth has a purpose, a purpose based
upon a realistic view of life and of themselves, and one
so oriented that any new knowledge, either of men or of
things, can only help and not injure that purpose.  Italian
youth has for the moment been given a purpose in the
building of a Fascist state, and German youth has put
its idealism into the building of a National-Socialist state.
But this does not greatly help for two of these efforts
must end tragically, either in serious disillusionment,
bitterness and cynicism, or in slaughter on a national
battlefield.  Perhaps the Italian or the German boy who
dies heroically in battle, before his ideals have shown
tarnish, will be the fortunate boy.  The boy who will
suffer will be the boy who lives on to disillusionment.
And there must be disillusionment.  For Fascism in
Italy and National-Socialism in Germany are based upon
the same unrealities as was the society against which
these movements are a rebellion.  They are no more real
than were the societies which they have replaced.  They
can accomplish nothing except to make superficial changes
upon the surface of things.  And the effort, honest
though it may be, can only lead to a retardation in social
progress with greater confusion, cynicism, and discouragement.  In the other countries of Europe, youth is as much
without a purpose as youth in America.

More important than that these youths shall pass their
courses in mathematics or satisfy the other requirements
for a university degree is it that they shall find some
purpose that will make significant the doing of these
things and living itself.  It may be too much and the
result another " lost generation ", too bewildered to find
any direction.  The very fact, however, that some have
called a halt in what is expected of them, that they at

least feel and often see the fallacies in our own living gives reason to believe that they may work through to positive values.  Dealing with an old structure, recognition that it is now useless and ready for replacement is the first step in construction.  In all this they probably cannot expect much help from us.

It will require probably more than is possible for us merely to keep out of their way.  We would like to help, however, not in just this negative way, but in a positive way.  But our impulse does not take into consideration what to help would entail.  A mere glimpse of what it will mean even to follow these youths, let alone helping them, will be enough for most, even enough to arouse an opposition that youth will then have to expend energy upon in destroying.  As the young woman student who felt it necessary to protect the sex innocence of her mother,[1] youth may find it better to protect us from knowing too much.

The job of these youngsters will not be to arrange schemes for various kinds of pensions and insurances, and this and that, in an effort to take a little from this one in order that another may have a little more.  The job will be to cut through the jungle of unreal philosophies, ideas, ideals and codes, that have produced the conditions that require all this " planning ", to a solid state of reality upon which new codes can be built.  In this cutting away many of the things that we have held to be most precious and most vital must go, at least in the form in which we have held them.

If we could but see that the change is in the form rather than in the thing itself it would help us.  But that is very difficult to see, and any attack upon the form in

[1] p. 151.

which the thing is held arouses our anxiety because we
believe it is the thing itself that is being destroyed. This
only shows how uncertain we are that those things which
we have held vital and fundamental and, therefore, really
indestructible, are vital and fundamental. Did we really
have faith in the fundamental nature of these things that
we insist so strongly are fundamental, we would be less
disturbed by changes in their form.

As we have said, " God " and " Service " in the form in
which we have used them have no significance to present-
day youth. And the most damaging thing that could be
done would be to try to revive these concepts for youth.
These must now take their historic place with the Greek
gods and the other gods on the one hand and with the
ideas of loyalty to a feudal lord on the other. They are
false in the form in which we have held them and any
social order raised in consequence of their revival can
only be a form of Fascism. Youth must get nearer than
this to what is real. These ideas, in the form in which we
have held them, youth must destroy and we stand in the
way, sometimes directly across the path, more often and
more dangerously as we sit as comrades in their camp
and poison the stream of their thoughts.

A minister of a " fundamentalist " school of religion
declares in a commencement address that the Industrial
Recovery Act is " contrary to the Bible, and hence evil ",
and continues " that it would be far better for labourers
to work at lower wages six days a week than to waste their
time in idleness ", and that " legislation to bring about
shorter hours and higher wages is calculated to over-
throw one of the laws of God ".[1] A more eminent minister

[1] " Finds Short Work Week is Contrary to the Bible ", *The
New York Times*, July 2, 1933.

who comes from Scotland to address a conference of
ministers and other Christian workers at the Union Theological Seminary in New York, in warning against the
" new morality ", as typified by certain modern writers,
speaks " of a loving, caring Father-God ". This is bad,
immoral talk and there must be an end to it eventually.
He continues even more destructively, " We admit that
we are animals, but we are more than animals—we are
reasoning spirits." [1] The promulgation of such ideas is
far more destructive to youth trying to find a way than
volumes of pornographic literature. The Primate of
Spain in a pastoral letter to the Spanish bishops and
people on the " expulsion of God from his country " says,
" Even pagans agree that God is the best social safeguard
and that the expulsion of God means the ruin of a people.
Without God there is no justice, fidelity, charity nor confidence. The immorality of the public coincides with the
absence of God." [2] This, too, is shockingly immoral for
the public prints. However, none of these represents
very serious danger to youth with the possible exception
of the one statement of the minister from Scotland.
Most of it falls of its own weight, and the world moves
along. Far more dangerous than the " fundamentalist "
is the " modernist " preacher who has thrown overboard
all that was least harmful—because so childish and absurd
—but has retained the false and unreal concepts which
were the foundation of what he has thrown over and
which have a logical and intelligible expression in funda-
mentalism, but which carry the potential of great social

[1] " ' New Morality ' Seen as Return to Jungle ", *The New
York Times*, July 20, 1933.
[2] " Primate of Spain Fears for Church ", *The New York
Times*, July 19, 1933.

disorganization and destruction when an attempt is made to express them otherwise.

There were few readers, I am sure, who were not thrilled by the report [1] of the courageous address made by Sherwood Eddy in Berlin before a gathering of German officials and leaders of business and the professions, in which he discussed forthrightly some of the things happening in the Nazi Germany. Mr. Eddy, formerly secretary for Asia of the Y.M.C.A. and for a number of years a leader of travelling seminar groups of students, educators, and professional men, studying social conditions in various countries, is reported to have deplored the new German attitude toward liberalism and racial problems. The report continues :

" We are glad to note the signs of progress, of advance and of achievement in the new Germany," he said in part. " There is manifestly a new national unity, a new enthusiasm, a call for a youth movement, a new spirit of hope and of self-help, and the first signs of economic recovery, as in the United States.

" I speak as a lifelong friend of Germany, but I also speak as a friend of humanity.

" We are on our way to Russia to study that great experiment in building a new social order. The Russians point to many achievements, but we find three serious defects or failures or evils as yet in their system.

" There is a denial of impartial justice with its substitute of class justice and the crushing of every foe. There is a denial of liberty, which is called a bourgeois prejudice. And there seems to be a denial of certain fundamental laws or principles in moral and economic life which have been found of value in human experience. . . .

" We are concerned with these same three principles in

---

[1] " Eddy Assails Nazis at Berlin Meeting ", *The New York Times*, July 21, 1933.

the life of Germany as in Russia.  Are you giving impartial justice for all, or merely class or racial justice for the Nordics and favoured Aryans ?  Have you given justice to the Social Democrats, to the despised Communists, to the Jews and to the liberals ?

" Second, have you given liberty of thought, of conscience, of speech, of the press, of association ?

" The Archbishop of Canterbury presided at a mass meeting of unanimous protest against Germany's treatment of certain classes and groups.  But was it published in your press ?

" Columns of self-criticism are welcomed in the press of Russia by labouring men.  But if you hold criticism to be treason and confine the press to the official propaganda of one party alone, you will never know what is going on in the rest of the world nor even in Germany itself.  Only to-day people have come to us asking us to tell them what is going on in Germany.

" Your laws tend to the extermination of the Jews.  Here in a daily paper yesterday is an article on ' Why the Influence of Judaism Should Be Broken '.  Here in my hand is a textbook used in your schools where hatred and contempt for the great Jewish race are instilled into the children of Germany.

" I have myself listened to your orators preaching flaming hatred of the Jews, which was mighty likely to have incited their hearers to pogroms.

" I do not speak of atrocities.  Those occur in all wars and in the beginning of all revolutions and are always exaggerated in the stories about them.  But much more serious is economic elimination, which may lead to the starvation of this despairing people.

" I had hoped to find that there was no longer persecution of the Jews.  Instead I have learned from many reliable witnesses, both Jew and Gentile, that the fate of the German Jews is becoming increasingly more hopeless.

" If we cannot excuse or deny or defend the lynching of our Negroes in the United States, although fortunately it is decreasing, you cannot defend or deny the sad fate of all these races and groups and classes.

" I see no hope until together we return to and follow the principles of impartial justice, equal liberty for all and those fundamental principles of moral and economic life upon which the past progress of the human race has been founded."

The report concludes with a paragraph that should not be omitted here.

The reception dispersed in a flurry as soon as Mr. Eddy had concluded his speech, and Herr Draeger, the president of the Karl Schurz Society, forgot to pronounce the customary benediction in the surprise provoked by the address.

Our response to the dramatic setting of this address and to the straightforward and manly nature of the address itself, makes it difficult for us to defend ourselves against some of the ideas themselves, but it is of the greatest importance that we do defend ourselves, for these ideas, not as applied specifically to Nazi Germany, but as ideas in general, are most destructive ideas. The paragraph :

" I see no hope until together we return to and follow the principles of impartial justice, equal liberty for all and those fundamental principles of moral and economic life upon which the past progress of the human race has been founded,"

is far more destructive as it stands than pornography or the immoral literature of " fundamentalists ". Words are accepted for actualities. What can be given a name, is said to exist. It is an adoration of symbols, even in the presence of the death of the things symbolized. Nothing is more destructive than such confusion. Youth must come to distinguish between words and things, symbols and actualities.

No such thing as impartial justice or liberty for all exists in any part of the world to-day or ever has existed.

It is idle to talk as though it had or that we make progress towards it. The form of injustice or the form of slavery has changed from age to age, or even from generation to generation, but injustice and slavery have remained. And there is nothing in our present social order, bulwarked by such high-sounding but self-deceiving sentiments as mentioned above, that ever can eradicate them, or even make progress towards eradicating them ; can ever do more than merely to change the form. There are those who have been able to see that the social order that we have erected upon a foundation that is unrelated to life and to men, as they are, is in itself so utterly false, because of its even greater lack of relation to life and men, that it can indeed only increase these things. It is the very foundation of our social order that needs attention, not the flimsy part of the superstructure that receives so much attention. And in getting at this foundation, ripping it up and rebuilding it, we must go directly to the job, and the thing that will hamper us most will be this tendency to accept the word for the deed.

The tragedy in Germany is not the loss of impartial justice or of equal liberty for all, which never did exist, but that the violent increase of injustice and illiberality can serve no useful purpose, but entrenches more firmly the same social order, on the same false foundation. The loss of those things which are called " impartial justice " and " equal liberty for all ", but which in reality are no such things, to the end of ripping up these foundations and rebuilding them, in such way as to give prospect of bringing actual impartial justice and real equal liberty for all, would be no loss and no tragedy, but a social gain.

There is an important difference between ruthlessness

in Germany and ruthlessness in Russia.   To say merely
that ruthlessness is ruthlessness and force is force is again
merely to deal with words ; but we have ever to deal with
actualities, not words.   To drive a Jew from his shop in
Germany is merely that another, for the moment more
favoured person, may take his place ; the social principle
that underlay the existence and the work of the shop
remains the same.   To drive a Jew (and all others as well)
from his shop in Russia is that no one may ever again
take his place, and that the social principle upon which
the shop was maintained shall be destroyed.   Sherwood
Eddy has made many trips to Russia, and as he has
stated, not only in the address quoted here, but often,
approves what has been accomplished there, but finds
things that wound his sensibilities.   In war and revolution, one may expect to have his sensibilities wounded.
The important thing is what significance one attaches to
this wounding.   One can attach such importance to it
as to be unable to see the significance of what has wounded
him.   He is then likely to fall back upon the easy worship
of words, abstractions and empty symbols, ignoring
entirely the living things about him.   It is important to
dwell upon this here, not as criticism of Sherwood Eddy
whom one can admire on many scores, but because
Sherwood Eddy is representative of the feeling and thinking (one uses " feeling " advisedly) of a large group of
individuals most attractive to many youths, attractive
because of their idealism, of their social vision, their
fair-mindedness (as these youths judge these things), their
intelligence combined with a courage that challenges but
does not challenge too much, which gives an opportunity
for tempered revolt, feelings and words of revolt but
calls for no great sacrifices, even provides warmth of

feeling through companionship.  With words and logic these men daily make gold from lead, make incompatibles compatible, lions and lambs lie down together.   For three or more generations they have shown that there is no conflict between science and religion when there is an unending conflict to the death between these two things. Redefining religion in terms of science is merely a dodging of the issue and an acknowledgment of the fact.   Since the field of interest has moved from religion to economics, these same men now try to show us that there is no real conflict between labour and capital and that a spirit of co-operation can smooth away all difficulties, when, as a matter of fact, there is an unending conflict to the death between these two, first, because men are what they are as men (which is something quite different from what the philosophers think) and, in the second place, because these very philosophies have made us all " capitalists " and the conflict, therefore, even more intense.   The most difficult task before youth is to arouse itself from the narcotics of words and logic, to realize that these instruments are as dangerous as they are valuable, and that they have no value and are lethal except when used in relation to actualities.

Sherwood Eddy's report that much has been accomplished in Russia but—" There is a denial of impartial justice with its substitute of class justice and the crushing of every foe ;  there is a denial of liberty which is called a bourgeois prejudice ;  and there seems to be a denial of certain fundamental laws or principles in moral and economic life which have been found of value in human experience "—contains the same confusion as there would be in the report of a war correspondent who sent word that the army with objective after objective won was approaching its goal but that it was using very large guns, spoiling a lot of country-side and killing an awful lot of people.   Either we disapprove the objects for which the war is being fought and must refuse to condone the loss of one man, or we approve the objects that are being fought for and shall have to accept the temporarily spoiled country-side and the death of people.

" The crushing of every foe."   Who are these foes ? Why are they crushed ?   If it is admitted that for our objective we must and may crush our foes, how are we to do it nicely ?   On what basis are we to differentiate between our foes ?   Are we to crush only the weak ones ? —but they have as much right to consideration as the strong ones.   Are we to crush only the strong ones ?— but they have as much right to consideration as the weak ones.   And anyway who makes a foe and the kind of foe that must be crushed ?

" A substitution of class justice for impartial justice." Where would it be possible to substitute a class justice for an impartial justice, except as one assumed that a word was the same as a fact ?   To say that in Russia in the process of moving towards something else the justice of one class had been substituted for the justice of another class, would have meaning, but the statement as made does not express the Russian concept of justice.   It is as though one were to condemn a city for its hog-wallow streets at a time when the city, as no other city, was busily occupied in putting its streets in order, and at the same time to complain of the necessary inconvenience caused by the process of laying the streets.   Or it is as though one were to say that this ancient structure, which covers many blocks of territory, must in the interests of all come down.   You may take it down, but in the process you are to make no noise, no dust, and in no way to change the appearance of the landscape, or disturb anyone who must work or sleep in the vicinity.   It gets back finally to " Hang your clothes on a branch of a tree, but don't go near the water."   " A denial of liberty which is called a bourgeois prejudice ", precisely ;  but not liberty, only such preoccupation with a word that illiberalities mount while conferences are called to make note of social progress.

Youth is not faced with a football match in which all will play hard but will remain gentlemen.  Present-day youth comes upon the scene at a time when issues are sharper, clearer, better defined than at any other time, and when conflict cannot be avoided.   It will be a sharp, hard conflict or a longer, agonizing conflict.  Which it will be will depend upon the extent to which youth can free itself from us and, digging up the actualities we have attempted to bury, grapple with them.

# CHAPTER VIII

## CAN RUSSIA CHANGE HUMAN NATURE?

HUMAN nature can't be changed—that is the challenge of many to all that is being tried in Russia. But returning from a second visit I must brush that assertion aside as too naïve. I believe that I have seen evidence of amazing changes in human beings. These must be accounted for. If important changes are taking place and if human nature can't be changed, then—what is human nature?

We have been suspicious of this " human nature " business before, but only vaguely so. Now it bursts on us. What after all do we know about human nature? As a matter of fact we know a great deal. But where did we get this information? What individuals have we studied? Individuals in what setting? Always in one setting. Whether in this country or that, this part of the world or the other, it has always been in the same setting. We have studied individuals in a class-organized, competitive society. We have studied individuals in such a setting only. We have no data outside this setting. (Studies of primitive peoples do not alter this statement.) We have reason to believe that our knowledge is accurate and to trust it, but does what we know explain " human nature " ? Is it anything more than human nature in a certain setting? Are we not like the man who, examining the world as he stands upon the prairie, insists there are no mountains, or another who travels here and travels there and from the only experience he has insists that the world is flat?

What happens to this " human nature " we know so well and work with so much in an entirely different setting? One way of getting at this, at least, will be through examining efforts and results in promoting mental health in the different settings of Russia and the United States. What is Russia's civilization doing in terms of the goals we have set for ourselves: preventing nervous and mental disease, diminishing the amount of delinquency, placing round and square pegs in round and square holes in industry, increasing happiness in marriage, diminishing the number of maladjusted school children, finding more adequate adjustment for the adolescent and, looking toward the future, guarding the emotional development of children?

The rate of incidence of nervous and mental disease in Russia is falling. At least there is evidence that warrants the belief that this may be so. It is too early yet for figures. But that there is the slightest evidence of this possibility is nothing less than staggering. No one would be so bold as to prophesy when there will be a drop in the rate here—not even if given the range of three generations in which to work his prophecy. The cautious will wait for a five-year set of figures before taking seriously such a statement with reference to Russia. Some of us, however, are interested in knowing how the wind is blowing as well as in knowing of the fact after the fact.

As is commonly known, Russia is building many new cities out on the steppes in the vicinity of new factories. Into these cities pours a population of forty, fifty, sixty thousand people, mostly peasants who never have lived or worked under such conditions. One of the important problems for Russian medicine has been to determine the hospital needs for these cities.   In a city of fifty thousand people, how many beds will be required for surgery, for internal medicine, for obstetrics, for gynæcology, for pediatrics, and with the rest, for nervous and mental disease?   It is a problem similar to the one faced by American medicine at the time the United States entered the War—in a cantonment of a certain number of men, within a certain age range, how many beds will be required for this, that or the other medical specialty?

There are recognized ways of computing these figures and the estimate made for the American army in regard to the number of beds that would be required for nervous and mental disease turned out to be accurate.   Any state with an adequate statistical bureau, such as New York or Massachusetts, can estimate the number of beds the state will require ten years from now.   Using the same method and making their calculations upon previous Russian experience, the number of beds for nervous and mental disease that would be required in the hospitals of the new cities was calculated.

Having determined their figure the Russian psychiatrists were considerably concerned that the figure might turn out to be an under-estimation, as the people for whom they were providing were superstitious and ignorant peasants, totally unfamiliar with city or industrial life.   Many of them had never before seen an iron wheel or an inside water-closet; they never had lived or worked under conditions even approximating to those under which they were about to come, and surely this stress and strain would break them down more rapidly than the usual rate of breakdown shown by the figures.   However, the beds were provided in accordance with the figures.

The beds are ready—but they are in large part unoccupied. The wards are operating far below their capacity. The Russian psychiatrists are themselves surprised, even startled. What should the emotions of an American psychiatrist be? These " crazy " people apparently won't even go crazy when they should!

Had the next statement come to me casually or second hand I should not repeat it as it seems too far beyond possibility to be given credence. It comes, however, from Dr. L. Rosenstein, director of the Scientific Institute for Neuro-Psychiatric Prophylaxis in Moscow, in whom I have confidence. With amazement that showed that it was difficult even for him to believe his own experience, he told me that he had been searching the hospitals of Moscow for three months for a new case of manic-depressive depression to demonstrate to his students and had not been able to find one. This is about like saying one has been searching in vain for an apple tree in an orchard. Probably enough cases of this type have been admitted to any one of the mental hospitals in New York City this very day to furnish demonstration material to all the medical schools of the city and possibly several other cities besides.

In September, 1931, there were five large prophylactoria for prostitutes in Moscow—institutions where former prostitutes were cared for during a period of re-education and re-training as citizens in Russia's new industrial order. It was estimated that the problem of prostitution might be " liquidated " within two years. The expression " within two years " did not seem to indicate exactly twenty-four months but to mean a comparatively short period. Ten months later, on my return, four of these prophylactoria had been closed because they no longer were needed and power machines for stocking-making used in re-training the women had been transferred to the hospitals for mental disease.  There remained one prophylactorium.  Essentially the problem was " liquidated ".

Although a divorce may be obtained in Russia in ten minutes by either party with no reason required other than that the party desires a divorce, the divorce rate is said to be falling.  It may have been a coincidence, of course, but I was unable to " show " a divorce to friends last summer.  Marriages we saw, but no divorces.  A year ago one never failed to see several divorces in the course of a two-hour stay at a marriage and divorce bureau.

I believe it can be stated that delinquency in our sense is not a major problem in Russia.  Even political crime, counter-revolutionary efforts by representatives of what is left of old Russia, gives less concern, although the government remains alert.  There was an epidemic of petty stealing during the summer, particularly bothersome in the West and South-West, and it was interesting to see what attitude the Russians took in regard to it.  There was no endeavour to hide it.  The stranger was not left to discover it.  It was impressed upon him from the first that this stealing was going on and that he must protect his things.  The explanation ?  " Of course there is stealing.  We have been unable to supply to some all that they require in the way of clothing, shoes and the like because of shortage in these things.  Under these conditions some people will steal.  The rise of this stealing is coincident with this shortage and will stop, except for isolated instances, as soon as we can furnish all people with what they require.  Our effort now is to do this. In the meantime, however, watch out for your things."

I found no evidence that maladjusted school children are a serious problem in Russia. There are difficult children, to be sure, but the number is not sufficiently great to absorb any large part of anybody's time. This is not neglect nor failure to see a problem. Of one thing the Russians cannot be accused and that is lack of alertness in spotting a problem.

When you ask about " adolescent problems " they do not understand what you mean. If you illustrate by a case, the case is recognized at once, but no problem. To be sure, they have such adolescents but again not in sufficient numbers to constitute a " problem ".

Obviously I have not seen every family in Russia and I am not prepared to say that Russian parents do not have difficulties with their children. There is a simple way, however, in which one can get some idea about their family life and in a kind of setting familiar in the West— the family parties in the Parks of Culture and Rest. These parks are in every city and in Leningrad or Moscow, Tiflis, Rostov, Yalta, Odessa, Kiev or where else, one has an excellent laboratory for observation. We are familiar with family holiday excursions to the park or to the country. It is usually a day of tension for the children and not much of a *re-creation* for the father or mother. Evening all too often finds the family nervously exhausted and quarrelsome. The thing I noticed at once in these Russian family groups was the lack of tension between members of the family. The very small children have been left in the park nursery or kindergarten, the older children are with the parents. The relationship that seems to exist between the parents and child attracts one at once. There is a genuine friendliness. These parents seem actually to like their children and the children seem actually to like their parents. Obviously they are having a good time together. At the end of the day, as they move towards the park exits, or crowd into trams, or walk along the street, they still seem in the same friendly humour towards one another and still to be having a good time together.

This same lack of neurotic tension is to be noted in the crowds of young people out for a walk of an evening on the main street of such towns as Rostov or Tiflis or the summer resort towns along the Black Sea such as Yalta. They are composed of men and women mostly between the ages of eighteen and thirty-five. They fill the sidewalks to the curbing, two and two, or in groups. They are alert, they walk along with a healthful vigour— as one observes them the words " petting " and the like do not come into one's mind but rather *joie de vivre*. There is the hum of talk, there is laughter, but there is no nervous tension in the neurotic sense. There is no rushing about, no pushing and shoving, no screaming, no shrill laughter or high-pitched speech, no horseplay, no boisterousness. Even in the towns on the Black Sea where many of them are patients in sanatoria for physical illness of one kind or another, they seem to be young people with thoroughly healthy nerves, out for a good time and having it thoroughly. There is none of the stridency or hysterical tension of our young people at Coney Island or in public parks generally.

Let us look back on our own efforts during the past twenty years to make people happier, healthier, more satisfactory members of society by means of what we know as mental-hygiene activities. Our method has been clinical, that is, working personally, individual by individual, each individual a special " case ". With us " mental hygiene " is largely a professional matter and we have developed for it a professional personnel. The work belongs essentially to the psychiatrist, working with his specialized knowledge in the social field. The psychiatrist has been supposed to know what is " psychically " wrong with people and what is " psychically " good for people.

In the course of time two points of view have developed, the one strongly professional with resentment against anyone else presuming to know, often even when that person is a person of considerable training and experience, such as a psychologist or a psychiatric social worker ; the other a professionally directed undertaking but including the co-operation of specially trained persons such as psychologists and psychiatric social workers, with an endeavour to bring into the field of co-operation, parents, school teachers, nurses and all others who come in contact with children, by infiltrating into these groups the " psychiatric point of view ". In the one instance, the doctor diagnoses and prescribes and has his orders carried out by assistants precisely as he would do in his hospital ; in the other, the doctor is as much or more an educator as a physician and endeavours to prepare others to diagnose and to treat, so that the simpler problems can be treated in a simple way and the more complicated with the degree of expertness they require, the most complicated remaining still to him. Both, however, represent the effort of a special professional group or groups to make an impression upon the social body. While a part of that body, they at the same time remain exterior to it.

The results that we have obtained in the field of mental

hygiene are not in the least to be minimized. The programme is intelligent and logical. Results would be
expected first with individuals and these results, in spite
of certain failures, have been excellent on the whole. An
appreciable social result, all realize, could come only
slowly. Gradually, with the infiltration of mental-
hygiene principles into the various fields of human activity
and association, results on a social scale could be expected.
As a matter of fact this infiltration, particularly into the
fields of delinquency, education and parental relationships, has taken place much more rapidly than anyone
had a right to expect. The point of view towards human
behaviour of leaders in all these fields has been or is
definitely changing. This is an important accomplishment but not a solution, and as one considers the one
hundred and twenty million people in America, parents,
teachers, children, one can think only in terms of generations as one thinks of lessening the incidence of mental
disease, for example, or appreciably lowering the rate of
delinquency.

We must admit, and it is no criticism of the plan to
admit, that as yet no appreciable social result has been
obtained in any field of mental hygiene. The incidence
of mental disease continues yearly to rise. It shows not
even a tendency to fall. The rate of delinquency increases
(except possibly juvenile delinquency); the rate of
divorce increases. While no figures are kept to indicate
the number of maladjusted children, or the number of
adolescents in difficulty (short of official delinquency),
no one in touch with these fields would say that there
was any diminution of these problems. And no informed
person expects any diminution in any of these problems
for years to come. This is not to say that the mental-

hygiene programme is a failure and worthless. The mental-hygiene programme is intelligent and excellent and will bring results. It is a programme built upon knowledge and designed for co-ordination into a certain social structure. The social structure remaining what it was, I can conceive of no better programme. And if the social structure remains as it was, wisdom will dictate placing all possible strength behind the mental-hygiene programme with the expectation that there will gradually evolve a sufficiently stable individual to bring a diminution in the social problems that trouble us so seriously to-day.

Could the events since 1914 be wiped out, had nothing happened in the social world since then, had the world continued on its slow evolutionary way, mental hygiene could have evolved with it. But the experiences of these years cannot be wiped out. Things have happened and we are not permitted to go peacefully on our way. One of the things that has happened is the beginning of the building of a new civilization in Russia. Things have happened there of which we cannot fail to take note. So much has happened, in fact, that we are challenged to compare our methods in the field of mental hygiene and twenty years of organized work with the methods in use in Russia and the results of a few years of work. Ordinarily we would think that to compare twenty years of work with a much shorter period would hardly be fair. The pace of events in Russia, however, forces us to do this and we need have no feeling that it is unfair. We cannot even compare our twenty years with the fifteen years of the present régime in Russia since during that time Russia has seen war, revolution, civil war, invasion, famine and serious social disorganization. Most of these years have gone into getting ready to begin. The Russians are still in the process of building a communistic state and are far from their goal. What a communistic state will mean in human terms it is impossible to know, but in the few years of comparative social order and organization enough has happened to make one wonder and at least to challenge a comparison with what we have accomplished in twenty years.

If, from what I have said, it would appear that Russia is a place where all problems of human relationship have been solved, where there exists no nervous or mental disease, no delinquency, no marital difficulties, no child-parent difficulties, no adolescent problems, no maladjusted school children, one should disabuse oneself of any such idea at once. What I can say is this—that each of these is a problem of major social importance in the United States to-day, and that we have made little or no impression upon them in twenty years of mental-hygiene work ; that these same problems in Russia either are not major social problems or that a deep impression has been made upon them and there is evidence of a recession. And this is much less than twenty years.

One is staggered at first because one who has been working in these fields and who feels that he knows something about human nature knows that such things are impossible. But one has butted one's head so often against the wall of the " impossible " in Russia that after a time one ceases to brush aside the impossible so casually and endeavours rather to discover why the impossible has become possible. And there are reasons. It is not an accident. In a chapter, " The Psychologic Bases of Soviet Success ", that I have prepared for *The New Russia ; Between the First and Second Five-Year Plans*, I have tried to show what it is in the Russian social organization that might account for these results.

In the end it gets down to this : that it would be well for us not to be too sure that what we know as " human nature " is *human nature*. We are forced to conclude that what we know about human nature is what we have learned by studying *human nature in captivity*. We haven't been aware of this. We have been studying monkeys in a zoo and we know a lot about how they will perform in their zoo, but there is a limit to how much we can deduce as to how they will react outside the zoo.

In captivity people react with nervous and mental disease, with delinquency ; they prostitute themselves, they narcotize themselves with alcohol, they seek escape through religion, romance, illusion, " culture ", they gouge out each other's eyes and then feel very sorry about it and sentimentalize ; relationships that should be helpful and stimulating become baneful and depressing, others that should give deep satisfaction disintegrate and become painful—and this not with occasional individuals but with such large numbers as to constitute social problems. Outside captivity they do not seem to react in just the same way, except in individual instances not sufficient to create a " problem ".

In the first instance, have the problems developed because of certain inherent factors in human nature or have they been created by the process of captivity ? In the second instance has " human nature " been changed or merely been permitted to be something more nearly like itself ? Is it possible that we are still in the position of the doctor of earlier generations who treated his typhoid patients conscientiously one by one, to the best of his ability and, when they died, had to attribute the

failure to individual weakness or the working of provi-
dence ? It undoubtedly seemed wholly " natural " to
such a doctor that a certain number of people should have
typhoid each year and a certain number should die.
Since his day modern public-health work has showed us
that it is possible to clean up the sources of typhoid in a
community, making it unnecessary for anyone, except by
rare accident, to have typhoid or to care for typhoid.
We have learned that typhoid is not a " natural " phe-
nomenon but a disease passed on by the sick to the well,
hit or miss, when the community fails in its management
of common concerns.   At least this fact stands out boldly
in a contrast between Russia and America—in Russia
mental hygiene is inherent in the social organization, in
America such mental hygiene as we have is injected into
the individual and the social body by a group of professional experts in " human nature ".

Russians, being human beings, cannot be essentially
different from the rest of us.   A developing Russian child
has the same psychological problems to solve as a child
of any other nation, and the way in which these problems
are solved will determine his later relation to others and
to social life generally.   To use psycho-analytical terminology—and there is no other terminology to use—Œdipus,
castration, anal-erotic complexes, " masculine protest "
and " inferiority feelings ", and the like, are the basis of
an individual's psychic life in Russia as here, but what
happens to them ?   Something certainly, for individuals
reacting to the same things react very differently there
than they do here.   A part of what happens we can understand.   What remains to be understood constitutes a
problem of transcendent importance and one that should
give us no rest until it is understood.

## CHAPTER IX

### EDUCATION : CAN RUSSIA TEACH US ?

THOUGHTFUL people, educators, physicians, social workers ask repeatedly what we may learn from Russia. But I wonder if they understand what being taught by Russia means, and if they did, whether they would be willing to accept what Russia has to teach. We are familiar with the process of borrowing from, and exchanging with, other nations, new techniques. New methods are readily exchanged ; but we are not dealing here merely with another nation. We have to do with an altogether different civilization. We cannot learn from Russia as we can learn from other nations with a civilization similar to our own. Learning from Russia comes close to being a proposition of all or nothing.

If you wish to understand the educational system in Russia you will not learn by studying the educational system ; you will learn by studying the social system. It is the social system that gives the educational system significance. It is not so much what is being done in education in Russia, or how it is being done (technique, method), as the spirit in which it is being done. The spirit is a product of the social philosophy, and the social philosophy is essentially simple : *There shall be no exploitation.*

Until we understand this in all its significance, its ramifications and implications, we shall understand nothing

in regard to Russia.   Until we understand this in its full
significance, we are not in a position to learn from Russia.
All that Russia has to teach us, even in the field of
education, is this—the possibility of constructing a civilization in a world of fact rather than in a world of
fantasy, and a civilization in which there shall be no
exploitation.   All else, education, morals, social technique, are merely derivatives of this, and all of these
things as found in Russia have no significance apart from
this.

The Russian school is honest in its relationship to the
civilization in which it exists.   There is no difference
between life within the school and life outside the school,
no difference in principle, in aims, in moral or spiritual
values.   A child comes from the community into the
school and back again into the community without any
shock or wrench, without any need for moral, spiritual,
ethical or practical re-orientation.

The Russian school is not a place where one " prepares
for life " and from which one " graduates " into life.
The school is not apart from life.   It is life, and the
preparation it gives is but for an extension into a fuller
and larger life—but a life which the child has known from
the beginning.

The success of the teacher lies not so much in her
knowledge of teaching technique as in the fact that she
and the child and the family and the community are but
different parts of the same thing, and each so thoroughly
understands this and each other's purposes and place in
the scheme of things that they are able to work with a
maximum of common purpose and a minimum of cross
purpose.   Under such conditions it is frequently possible
for teachers inadequately trained by our standards to

attain results seldom possible for even our best-trained teachers.

Our schools stand in a dishonest relationship to the civilization in which they exist. They stand apart and superior. Life outside is ugly; within we attempt to make it idealistic and beautiful. Our hope has been that our children would somehow leaven the loaf and gradually make life outside the school better and more in accordance with life within the school; the result is that after one hundred and fifty years, American education has left us as vicious socially and as dishonest as we were before that education began. We are no nearer our idealistic social goal than one hundred and fifty years ago.

What happens to our children? Fortunately for the majority, more sophisticated than their teachers, they attend politely to what we say but ignore our teaching. They are not ruined by the school for the life they must live and leave the school reasonably well equipped to start the struggle that is before them. The finest, the most sensitive, probably the most capable of social contribution, are crushed or, after a terrific conflict, get " wise " and start playing the game according to the rules used in the outside world.

One does not succeed in this civilization if one takes too seriously the principles taught in the school. Leaders in the field of education itself are not necessarily those who have moulded their lives too closely by the ideals they were taught, and now teach. There is a great gap between the life in the school and life on the outside of the school.

It would be more honest and less confusing if schools taught the morals, the ethics practised in the civilization which supports them and of which they are a part. If the values within the school were the same as the values outside the school—there is only one principle common to both and that is the principle of personal ambition and getting on—it would be much less difficult and all would probably " get on " faster. So great is the difference between life outside the school and life within the school, however, that we must go to considerable and awkward lengths to protect the child from knowing too much of life as it is actually lived. Consider the significance of this—our lives, the life of the community, is *so far* out of keeping with our school-taught principles that we must protect the child from knowing our real lives or the life of the community. If the disparity were only an exception here and there—but the disparity is so general and so great that we dare not let them know. The members of the school board, the mayor of the city, the governor of the state, are all men and women, guided and motivated by the same principles as are taught in the schools—so the school child is led to believe. That this is not true is carefully concealed.

We would be shocked to contemplate making life within the school the same as life outside the school. Very well, then the school must remain dishonest in its relationship to the civilization in which it exists; it must continue preparing children for life in a world that does not exist and leave them to be crushed and destroyed by the world as it is or to throw over our teaching and save themselves, as many of us have saved ourselves.

There is another way out. If we cannot teach life as it is and have the same principles within as without, then we may teach life as it is, but attack it. Teachers do not dare to do that in any effective way. They are helpless in this situation. They would be utterly destroyed, individually and collectively, if they actually told the truth about life. This situation is bigger than ourselves. It is the *system as a whole* that is our difficulty. The difficulty is not with our education ; the difficulty is with the system, the *basis* of the civilization as a whole of which we are all a part.

Consider the professions, the flower of our education. The legal profession is a humiliation ; business is a disgrace ; the medical profession tends towards being an unsocial trade union ; the teaching profession, intimidated, cloistered, runners-away from life ; the clergy, inconsequential.

It is painful to say this, but the question is, is it true ? As a physician, I rise at once in defence. Medical men must protect their science and their personal interests or they would be destroyed. It is not that men within these professions are not worthy, that they are not as good as any men in Russia or anywhere else in the world. We know this is not true. It is not because we are as individuals unworthy, but because as individuals, and because as groups, we are caught in a net, and we are helpless.

Has Russia anything to teach us ?

Russia has done more in fifteen years to raise the moral standards of her one hundred and sixty million people than American education has done in one hundred and fifty years or the Christian church in 1933 years.

In spite of all the effort we have expended intellectually, emotionally, physically, in studying our various so-called social problems, in spite of the work of all of our committees and commissions, our social problems remain as serious as they were before our studies began.

Crime, with all that we have done, is a serious major

problem ; alcoholism remains a serious problem ; nervous
and mental diseases take their annual ghastly toll ; maladjusted school children and adolescents continue to be a
problem of great concern.    In Russia, believe it or not,
these things have ceased to be major social problems, or
are rapidly diminishing as such.    It is inconceivable—
but there it is.    The rate of incidence of nervous and
mental disease has risen in our country every year since
statistics have been kept and the work of some of us who
have been labouring in the field of mental hygiene for
the past twenty years has not changed that increase one-
tenth of one per cent.    And yet in Russia there is reason to
believe that the rate of incidence of nervous and mental
disease is dropping.

Has this been accomplished by some legerdemain ?    Is
it by some trick that delinquency is not a serious major
social problem, that alcoholism is steadily decreasing in
social significance, that mental and nervous disease is
dropping not only surprisingly but unbelievably, that
there aren't so many maladjusted school children, that
adolescence in Russia is not a serious problem ?    This
has not been accomplished by a trick that we can learn
and apply here.

The Russian teacher has an advantage of superior
teaching material—not that the Russian school child is
more intelligent than other children.    The Russian children, however, have several advantages, gained from the
society in which they have lived, that tend to make them
superior as teaching material.    First, the child has a
purpose, and to carry out his purpose he needs the school.
Second, he is fully aware that he is wanted, even more,
that he is needed and that there is a place for him in
the social scheme of things.    Third, he is not terrorized

by life; he has a zest for it. It is not difficult to guide such a child to the things which, for reasons of his own, he wants to know. The purpose of the child has not been created by idealistic speeches made to him by his teachers, but is derived from the opportunity for life that he finds all about him. Life does not confuse and terrify him for the reason that the principles upon which his social system is based—no exploitation, mastery of the world through knowledge, united effort in the interests of all— are easily comprehensible to him, agreeable to him, in fact, seem eminently sensible to him. Nothing seems impossible about them, least of all their comprehensibility. He is not confused further by the fact that the principles enunciated to him as a school boy are violated openly or clandestinely by almost every adult he is called upon to respect. Clearly, then, these are principles by which he can be guided.

By the time the Russian child enters school, his education is already well advanced. The school becomes the means of attaining knowledge to be utilized in a purpose that he finds developing within himself. School to the Russian child is not an invention of the devil. If there were no schools in Russia the Russian children would need to create them for their own satisfaction.

Can Russia teach us? If we attempt to learn from Russia, it will be the hardest lesson we ever have attempted. And yet it is simple. *What* is it? Not tricks of education, not special methods in handling delinquents or nervous and mental conditions. It is merely this: that a civilization cannot be based upon the principles of exploitation but that a civilization can be based on the principle of no exploitation. Everything else, education and all, follows from this.

# CHAPTER X

## WHAT ADOLESCENTS CANNOT UNDERSTAND ABOUT US

" Do you believe in co-education ? "

" Why, yes ; of course. Thoroughly."

" But we mean real co-education."

" Well, so do I, so far as I know. I assume you mean, Do I believe that men and women should attend the same colleges and classes ? "

" Oh, yes ; that, of course. But why do we live in separate dormitories ? "

" Why, indeed ? "

" Well, why ? Why should the girls not live here in this dormitory with us ? "

" You mean the girls on one floor and the boys on another ? "

" Well, that way, or as we wish. Why any distinction at all ? "

" But be sensible. What would happen under such conditions ? "

" Well, what would happen ? "

" You are good husky animals. Could you trust yourselves under such conditions ? "

" What do you mean, ' trust ourselves ' ? "

" Depend upon yourselves to behave yourselves."

" What do you mean by ' behave ' ? "

" You know very well what I mean by ' behave '."

" But why should we ' behave ' ? "

" What would your parents think ? "

" Well, what in the devil do they think ?   What do they think now ?   Do they do any thinking at all ? "

" There has been a good deal of thinking on the subject."

" And what does it all amount to ?   They say we should not masturbate as it is unnatural and indicates a weak will ; that we should not go with prostitutes because of disease ; that we should not have any ' unclean ' thoughts about ' nice ' girls.  Well, what are we to do ? "

" Exercise, athletics."

" Bosh ! "

" A bit more concentration on your work."

" Cart before the horse."

" But the purity of your women ? "

" Now, just what does that mean ?   And what are its advantages ?  A code that loses its value as soon as changed."

" But an epidemic of venereal disease ? "

" Why an epidemic of venereal disease ?  It doesn't follow.  It isn't necessary."

" Pregnancy ? "

" Why pregnancy ? "

" But have you no sense of fine feeling ?  You make common and vulgar what should be fine and beautiful."

" Of course we have a sense of fine feeling.  That's why we object to sneaking out behind bushes or inventing lies about trips."

" But your fathers and mothers controlled themselves."

" Did they ?  And if they did——? "

" Oh, well, now, come.  Let's be decent."

" Why be decent ?  Why not be honest ? "

" But your mothers ? "

" Let's not be sentimental.  My mother is a beautiful and attractive woman to-day and I'm sure she was an attractive and healthy young woman."

" My mother was one of the most popular girls of her day and she's the life of a party yet."

" I know about some of my father's affairs."

" So do I—and I don't blame him.  My mother is a fine woman, but sexually I think she has always been—what do you call it—cold, frigid ? "

" I don't think my parents have slept together for five years.  Mother loathes the whole subject of sex."

" There is something fundamentally wrong in the sex life of my parents.  Mother is neurotic and touchy ; poor old Dad has to sink himself in business.  I don't know how he manages it except that he uses all the energy he's got in making money."

" It's just the other way round in our family.  Mother is full of life and energy which she puts into running the town, that is church and social-service things.  Father's the one who lacks energy.  Mother's a good sport, a bit careless and slap-dash ; father's orderly and precise, almost prim.  I don't know why they ever got married."

" I don't know why my father ever married.  I don't think he gets any satisfaction out of it.  And it isn't mother's fault.  He just wasn't made for married life. He was ' innocent ', all right, I think, and a perfect example of youthful ' purity '."

" My mother was ' innocent ', all right, I'm sure of that. She was married at eighteen, and I think it was an awful shock when she found that marriage wasn't just dancing and parties.  Now everything seems spoiled for her.

She can't read, or go to the theatre or the movies ; she can't do anything because everything is sex, sex. Her only interest in life seems to be worrying over my sister and me for fear we will make ' mistakes '."

" But now wait a minute. Aren't any of your parents happily married ? "

" No."

" Come, that can't be so."

" They get along somehow—but they are not happy."

" Mine are divorced."

" So are mine."

" Mine have been talking divorce for two years."

" Mine should be divorced."

" Mine are so bitter against each other that neither would give the other a divorce."

" Mine love each other, I'm sure, but they just can't get together."

" It's the same with mine."

" But you put all the trouble on sex. There are many reasons why they might be unhappy—having to manage you and your sisters for one thing."

" No, it's sex. If they weren't themselves worried about sex, they wouldn't have to ' manage ' us—that's the managing they are really concerned about. They're all mixed up about sex."

" They have spoiled sex for themselves."

" They don't know it, but they would spoil sex for us in the same way."

" They talk romantically and live vulgarly."

And so they talk about these matters and about us. This is a part of a discussion that took place in a college dormitory and in which, as is apparent, I was put upon the defensive from the start—a somewhat unusual experience for me in liberal discussion. The discussion was not in the least vulgar or common. It was serious and thoughtful. Those who took part were freshmen and sophomores. The point they were apparently trying to make—I am still on the defensive; it is quite unfair to say, " the point they were apparently trying to make ", for they made their point quite clearly—was that they were asked to attend to their studies and in the process to forget what could not be forgotten; and this on the ground that anything else was socially and personally wrong; that it made common and vulgar what was sacred and beautiful; further, that they were to do this because presumably their parents had done so; and as a reward they were promised a later happiness which would otherwise be lost.

In their discussion of their parents there was no bitterness or cynicism—but a frankness that would appal most parents and a sympathy that would be embarrassing. The sexual lives of their parents were discussed as directly as if it had been their parents' taste in clothes or ability in golf. They could find nothing in the sexual life of their parents to commend. If there was a reward for continence in youth their parents had not reaped it. The sexual life of their parents was on the whole degrading rather than stimulating; it did not contain romance and beauty. Parents out of their experience had come to consider sexual life hateful and their attitude toward it had become vulgar. In spite of this they continued to urge their children to consider sexual life romantic and beautiful and to insist to the point of hysteria that they should look for this romance and beauty along the same road that they had come and precisely where they had failed to find it.

The boys themselves held strongly to the view of romance and beauty ; so strongly that they were determined to find it. They were convinced, however, that the road indicated by their parents was not the road to take —the failure of their parents was too obvious and the possible reason for the failure too apparent. The road was a road of ignorance and inexperience and of the fears engendered by ignorance and inexperience. Romance and beauty could not come out of such a situation. (All of which reminded me of a decision made by a young university woman in regard to her mother. From her work in sociology and psychology the young woman was not uninformed in regard to certain fundamental matters in sex. Attending on one occasion with her mother a popular lecture in psychology, the mother was puzzled by certain of the terms used by the lecturer and inquired of the daughter what they might mean. The daughter : " I told her what some of them meant, but as to others, it seemed to me that if mother had lived to be fifty years old and did not know about these things, then it would be better for her not to know at all. Why at this age disturb her innocence ? "—and this not cynically, but sympathetically. Formerly the parent protected the innocence of the child ; to-day the child protects the innocence of the parent.)

The young men did not fail to see the possible relationship between the ignorance and lack of sexual experience of their parents and their present state of sexual frustration. They were quick to grant, however, that their parents as youths had been faced with a much more difficult situation than were they. Venereal disease, pregnancy, and the influence of the church had made any course but continence exceedingly dangerous. With venereal disease understood, preventable, and curable, with conception in large part controllable, with sentiments based upon knowledge replacing the moral sentiments of the church based upon ignorance, their own situation was much easier. They had a chance where their parents had had almost none.

But this is only one situation in which our attitude is a puzzle and a stumbling-block to the adolescent.

The adolescent long ago gave up Santa Claus and fairy stories—did so, in fact, at our behest—and yet he finds us apparently still believing in them. Here is a contradiction difficult to explain. Do we or don't we believe in Santa Claus ? Are we to be considered hypocrites, liars, or just unintelligent ?

They do not seem inclined to use any of these terms, except when angry, for their attitude, on the whole, is quite generous. They are without a good term for us for they do not yet know that it is fear that makes us look and act like hypocrites, liars, and fools ; that we cling to our illusions because we do not dare to give them up.

The youth is inclined to accept a fact as a fact. Two and two are four. We have taught him that, he has checked it up himself and finds it correct, so we are agreed. That is, he assumes we are agreed, but only to find shortly another fact—that we aren't agreed at all, for two and two are four only when we like to have it so. And when we insist that it isn't so, it is always without being able to give any intelligent reason for it—only that for the moment we want it some other way. What is he to think ? He himself will probably stick to the original agreement and then think as well of us as he can. The difficulty is, of course, that he hasn't yet got to the stage

of " ifs ", " ands ", " buts ", and " possiblys " that tend
to make simple things apparently quite complicated.

He finds most of us believing little or not at all in the
supernatural doctrines of the church and yet pretending
and acting as if we did.   This seems curious to him.   If
the thing has served its usefulness, is outmoded, why
continue to support it ?   Why the economic waste and
the waste of energy ?   Why not construct something
useful in the way of a social ethics, perhaps, from what is
valuable and let the old forms go ?   It is to be noted here
that his bewilderment is not over the church but over us.
The question of the church as a social institution is one
that interests him and about which he forms opinions.
At the moment, however, he is engaged in trying to
understand our contradictory attitudes—disbelief (in
what we say), belief (in what we do by way of support),
or the reverse, disbelief (in what we do), belief (in what
we say).   He finds difficulty in making sense to it and
elaborate explanations are cut through at once with,
" Do you or don't you ? " and there is an implication
lurking about which seems to mean, " Are you an intellectually honest person or aren't you ? "

Economic questions interest him very much.   He sees
a world gorged with plenty and yet with people hungry ;
a social organization that gives so much to so few and
so little to so many.   And he asks simply, " Why is this
so ? "   Try and give him a long answer ; try and make
two and two not four.   Try and explain to him now what
you meant when you taught him that greed and selfishness were cardinal sins.   Unfortunately he took you at
your word, as in the case of two and two ; but apparently
you didn't mean it and now he is to join you in defending

a social organization built upon these cardinal sins. He is inclined to stick to the two and two and to wonder if you ever are honest. Honesty is another thing you taught him. Judging from what you do and say now, what did you mean then? Was that all just " kid " stuff, too, like Santa Claus and the fairies? Or do you really believe in Santa Claus? Perhaps it was wrong to have given up Santa Claus and the fairies.

Patriotism interests him ; at least, our attitude toward it does.

He has heard that in earlier days one's college, one's football team, one's fraternity were the greatest and only college, football team, and fraternity in the world. That was " loyalty " and one did almost anything in the name of loyalty from calling one's rivals hard names to fighting them or stealing from them. One hated one's rivals, or, at least, scorned them. " Michigan—bah ! " if one were from Wisconsin, or " Princeton—bah ! " if one were from Harvard. It was even hard to " love " one's own fraternity brothers in the other college when one made a trip with the team. Of course, unquestionably, one's crowd in the " foreign " college was the best crowd in the college—one not having seen any other crowd—but . . .

The youth of to-day has outgrown this childishness. He has quite definite concepts of loyalty, but he is beyond thinking that what is his is necessarily the best. He knows the strong points of his college, but this does not keep him from seeing its weaknesses and the excellences in other institutions. He is fond of his own fraternity group and prefers it to others, but he is quite aware of the good points of others. Childishness now and then breaks out, to be sure, but when it does he has withering expressions for it—" being collegiate " or " being all wet " —and a freshman once told, with the scorn that a junior can command, that he is " being collegiate " or is " all wet ", is likely to begin to grow up from that moment.

But when he returns home, he finds his parents and all the best people acting and talking like a callow fresh-man—or so it was until they began to talk about the " depression ".   The town is the " livest " in the state ; the local school system and water-works are the best in the world ;  the Christian religion is the only true religion ; the American social system is the finest in the world ; America's attitude on any international question is always fair, honest, and right ;  we are an idealistic, unselfish nation and all other nations are selfish ;  George Wash-ington never told a lie ;  Abraham Lincoln was a saint. And he isn't impressed.   It all seems being a bit " col-legiate ".

An analysis of youth's bewilderment over us and the confusion that arises as a consequence in his relationship with us makes clear the nature of the difficulty.   When we told him that two and two made four he offered no objection.   He saw how the calculation was made, could even demonstrate it for himself, and was satisfied.   The statement that *Alpha Centauri*, the nearest star, is 25,000,000,000,000 miles from the earth, or that, with light travelling at the rate of 186,000 miles a second, the most distant stars in the Milky Way are about 100,000 light-years away, that the surface temperature of a Type O star is about 35,000 degrees Fahrenheit, that the largest star, Antares, has a diameter of 415,000,000 miles, does not disturb him.   He may be appalled at such figures, but he is ready to accept them. He has not himself made these measurements and could not if he wished to, but he knows the principles upon which the calculations have been made and the methods used in calculation and, allowing for possible error in observation or calculation, he is quite willing to accept them until such time as new evidence makes necessary a change. He is quite willing to accept the statement, absurd as it may seem, that the most beautiful, sparkling spring water may contain the bacteria of typhoid fever. He has never seen a typhoid bacillus, or, if he has, he has never seen one in spring water. Nor can he demonstrate this for himself. But, again, he understands the principles and the methods that are used in determining such matters and is quite content to accept the results. He may have heard of such a thing as an " Œdipus Complex " and that this has much to do with determining the conduct of an individual whether he be the president of the university or a delinquent in the state's prison. He does not at once throw this out of court as absurd. Intangible as it may seem he is quite willing to consider it as a possibility, for again he knows how men have proceeded in arriving at this view.

In other words, no matter how strange, how seemingly impossible a statement may be, youth has no difficulty in accepting it, provided it is something we are able to say we *know*, in contradistinction to something we *think*, and if our knowledge has come in accordance with accepted procedures, the principles and methods of which he understands. The point at which he balks and where he begins to distrust us is the point at which we begin to assert (with a good deal of feeling) what we do not know ; where opinion, prejudice, feeling take the place of observation and calculation. We heatedly assert opinions—usually about religion, morals, ethics, human relationships—and frequently are enraged at the blank refusal such opinion receives. We are then inclined to begin to shout and to call names, from fool and nit-wit to " radical ". All of which leaves youth entirely cold. For much that we have asserted is blatant nonsense, much obviously untrue, much we know nothing about, much is patently dishonest. That which is none of these things, and which has marks of sincerity and sense, he is just as much at a loss to accept, since he has no way of knowing (and neither have we) by what process the judgment was reached. He must, therefore, continue to distrust.

The point of all this is not the superior wisdom of youth, except, perhaps, as a superior wisdom may come from a superior honesty, but to point out that in our difficulties with youth the right is not all on one side. If we have indictments to bring against youth, youth has serious indictments to bring against us, and a better relationship with youth will come not alone through correcting youth, but through correcting ourselves and thereby ceasing to be stumbling-blocks and obstacles that he must overcome. It is a rare father who is a fit companion for his son.

# CHAPTER XI

## THE CHILD'S NEED OF SECURITY

SECURITY is not alone a problem of childhood, it is a problem that concerns us all. Anxiety and fear are problems that all adults must themselves deal with in one degree or another and in one form or another. Often there is some factor in the world about us that causes this anxiety or fear. Often, however, if we are frank with ourselves, we can see that the amount of our anxiety or fear is out of proportion to the cause we have named. This anxiety or fear, or the excessive amount of it, is due to the insecurity within ourselves and has its roots in some of the things we wish to discuss here. We recognize our unnecessary or excessive anxieties and fears and worries as handicaps and it is these handicaps that we wish to avoid for our children.

Being born isn't the simplest thing in the world, when one comes to think about it. For nine months or at least for those months since the child has become physically aware of itself it has lived in an ideally comfortable world. It has swung easily and comfortably and without care in its human cradle, with all of its needs supplied without effort on its part, the supreme ruler, so far as it knows, of its universe—an ideal state of affairs, a condition of security and comfort which it will never attain again but will always desire. Suddenly there is a tremendous upheaval in its world and it finds itself wrenched and pulled, completely helpless in the overpowering forces about it, and it enters a world which, in spite of our best efforts, must seem a poor substitute for what it has known. If the child could express a desire at this time it would probably be to be returned to where it was and to be left alone. But not altogether this. There are forces within the child that make it want to live and to be more active. While it was secure and comfortable where it was comfort was growing less because it had outgrown its space and the forces within it were pushing for more activity like a sprout pushing its way up through the earth. A child at birth would therefore probably be of two minds, one desirous of the security and comfort without effort that it formerly had, the other desirous of kicking and stretching. This problem of being of two minds about what we want is never completely resolved. A part of us would always like to be secure and comfortable without any too much effort, while another part of us wants to push on, to have adventure and to exert ourselves in the overcoming of obstacles.

It is this problem of the division of wishes that constitutes one of the chief problems of childhood and the success in living of the adult individual will depend very much indeed upon how this problem is solved in childhood. It can be made so much worse that the adult is seriously handicapped or it can be sufficiently solved so that the adult is not seriously troubled. The solution will come through the wise guidance of the child through its developmental years. The child cannot be expected to understand the problem. All it can do is to react to its feelings at any given moment. As adults we can understand the problem and can, therefore, in our guidance of him help him by throwing the weight of our influence, at any given moment, to that element in the child's conflict that will be most constructive.  We know that in order to be happy and successful in living the child must develop from the completely dependent individual it is to a completely independent one.  Our efforts will be to assist it.

The mother as she holds her babe in her arms should know that a conflict *already* exists within the babe—a conflict between remaining secure with her and of becoming independent of her.  The need and desire to be dependent and secure with her will at first be the stronger. Having so recently come from a place of complete security, the adjustment to the new situation must be made as easy as possible.  At this period the child must be kept secure, for if in these early years the child becomes insecure serious problems arise that are difficult to solve.  A child that is seriously insecure during these early years is never likely to become a secure individual as an adult.  However, as the mother gazes at the babe in her arms the programme that forms in her mind should be that of gradually weaning the child from its dependency upon her until later in adolescence it can step out into the world strong and independent of her.  The emancipation of the child from the mother and the home should begin at birth and should not come in adolescence when a break must be made.  The child who has been led gradually to this point enters the world with comparatively little difficulty, whereas the child faced suddenly with the problem at adolescence is frequently thrown into serious panic and has great difficulty in making any suitable adjustment to the life that lies ahead of him.

The emphasis I would place is upon the gradual lessening of the dependence of the child.   Not infrequently parents who have learned of the difficulties caused by overcoddling children have gone to the other extreme and thinking that they were acting for the good of the child have persistently pushed the child away, as it were. This creates an equally serious situation in that the child does not have the security during these early years that it needs.   A young child must always be kept secure, that is, able to depend on the goodwill and affection of its parents, but step by step the dependency must be lessened.   The question as to what is too much or too little is not an easy one, but at the same time it is not one that should create overanxiety on the part of a parent.   It is what takes place in general over the period of childhood that counts rather than any mistaken moment here and there.   The best that one can do, perhaps, is to see as clearly as possible what one's plan for the child should be, and to understand those situations in which problems are likely to arise and the symptoms that the child is likely to show either when insecure or too dependent.

In a home where there is  goodwill and  affection between the parents the problem of insecurity is not so likely to arise.   The problem here is likely to be one of too great dependence upon the parents.   Insecurity is more likely to arise in broken homes, in homes where there is ill will and quarrelling between the parents. Insecurity will arise where discipline in a home is variable, where there is a serious difference between what the parents do and what they say, where children are deceived, are unfairly treated, where parents are dishonest, even intellectually dishonest, with their children, or break promises arbitrarily for reasons not understood by the child.   The birth of a second child is always a serious matter for the first child. The family's affection and attention go naturally to the new-comer and the older child is left seriously insecure. On all such occasions special attention should be given to the first child. A favourite child in the family makes all other children insecure. The favourite child at the same time becomes too dependent. A preference of the parents for boys or girls makes the unpreferred sex insecure. An unusually attractive or intelligent child challenges seriously the security of the other children in the group. Special attention should be given to the other children. An unwanted child is in an exceedingly difficult position. It is likely either to be seriously insecure or to become overdependent as the parents try to cover up the fact that it is unwanted. The greatest social stroke of mental hygiene would be if only wanted children were born.

A bad child is often nothing more than an insecure child. Where this is the case the solution is not punishment, which merely adds to the insecurity, but the making of the child secure by a show of attention and affection. This may seem a strange way to reward misconduct but where the misconduct is due to insecurity it is the only intelligent way. The extra attention or affection will not be given as a reward for bad conduct. If the conduct is not too serious it can be ignored or mildly reproved but the first opportunity will be sought to give the child some extra attention or affection. The wise parent will not wait for serious misconduct to develop but will prevent this by seeing what is happening to the child and will reassure the child of his affection—not by words but by acts—before a demonstration is necessary on the part of the child. A child who is becoming insecure may become rude, stubborn, cocky, rebellious, noisily overactive, and the like.   As one sees the restlessness of the child mounting one will—without particular comment on the conduct—offer the child some extra attention, spending more time with him to discuss his interests, making him a small present, taking him along on an errand, or whatever simple thing it may be, depending upon the age of the child, that will cause him to feel re-established in the affections of the parent.

An insecure child may show opposite signs.   He may become depressed, moody, and sulky, withdrawing into himself and doing a good deal of day-dreaming.   The remedy would be the same.

A too dependent child is likely to show a lack of initiative, selfishness, timidity, shyness, inability to get on with other children, fear of group activities.   Such children must be weaned away from their dependency and helped to find a security outside their parents.   They must not be " thrown out ", as this will create panic, but they must be steadily urged out.   This again not by words but by activity on the part of the parents in which they will make possible contacts outside the home.

An individual will not live his life with his parents, he will live it with his contemporaries.   It is well, therefore, for him to become accustomed to his contemporaries and learn how to get on with them at the earliest possible age.   A child raised alone is likely to become a seriously handicapped and pathetic adult.   Even where there are two, three, or four children in a family it is well for them to have outside contacts early.   Frequently the first outside contacts are made at six on going to school.   This is a serious mistake and places an unnecessary hardship upon the child.   The child's security must eventually come from the group and the earlier he learns to be a part of the group of his contemporaries the easier and better it will be for him. Parents often overprotect their children from the group for fear that the children will learn some bad words or uncouth manners, but a few bad words or some uncouth manners would be a cheap price to pay if in the process of gaining them the children were able to find the security in the group which will be important and determining for them for the rest of their lives. Probably the most tragic and pathetic people in the world are those with excellent manners and a polite vocabulary who find the world a very lonely place after their parents are gone.

What we should hope for in this programme of keeping the child secure at all times but at the same time gradually helping him to find his security outside the home and away from the parents would be an adolescent confident in himself but without boastfulness, with affection for his parents but without sentimentality, whose major interest lay outside the home in the various activities of his age, and who was comfortable in the presence of his own age group, both boys and girls. Such a boy or girl is ready to enter upon adult life a satisfaction to his parents and with excellent opportunity for satisfactory and successful living for himself.

Let me emphasize once more, however, that while parents should be serious about this matter they should not be too serious. They can use the best judgment they have, or if necessary they can seek advice. Mistakes are sure to be made but they need not be too serious. A child has much psychological resilience, as well as physical resistance to ills, and will recover reasonably well from many mistakes on the part of parents. And there can be this one comforting thought that no matter what mistakes we make the children will probably turn out no worse than ourselves.   Our parents made many more mistakes than we are likely to make with our greater knowledge.   We would like our children to be better than ourselves and less handicapped, but if worse comes to worse, and they are no better than ourselves, it will after all be no great tragedy.

## CHAPTER XII

### FEET OF CLAY

THE children of to-day may not be troubled by finding the same weaknesses in their elders that we as children discovered in ours, but they are still finding that even their parents do have feet of clay. The effect of their discoveries upon them seems possibly even more devastating than the results of ours upon us. In our childhood feet of clay were usually exposed in the field of sex morals; to-day they seem to be transferred to the field of economic morals. One cannot make too sharp a distinction here, but in general this seems to be true.

Most of the parents of to-day were children in the time when certain things were " wicked ". Sex was " wicked "; swearing was only less " wicked " than was a group of expressive four-lettered Anglo-Saxon words which one learned first from the scribblings on billboards and the walls of outhouses. At this time, too, alcohol had become a moral problem and " to drink " was also " wicked ". One not only learned early what " wickedness " was, but one also learned with equal finality that only wicked people did wicked things. And that classification excluded our parents for they obviously were not wicked. There were other people, too, who as they obviously were not wicked were excluded—the clergyman, the Sunday school superintendent, socially important men and women in the town, school-teachers, and most other people who were well dressed, polite and on the whole friendly.

To discover, then, that one's father liked an occasional glass of beer, " drank beer ", or that an idealized public character " went into a saloon " was indeed a blow. The worst blow, however, was on first learning about sexual intercourse. Facts first denied with revulsion later had to be accepted as a possibility but often with qualifications. " Your mother may do that, but mine doesn't." To hear someone, whom we considered perfect, and whom in our own weakness and " wickedness " we were trying to emulate, swear, or worse still, use one of the ghastly Anglo-Saxon words, was to have an idol totter on crumbling feet of clay. To learn that the vicar, when the young girl organist complained that the choirmaster had made improper advances to her, felt that the organist should be discharged instead of the choirmaster, could cause an adolescent heaven to fall with a crash that reverberated for a long time.

Under this philosophy the effort on the part of earnest parents was to " protect " children from knowing about what they considered the ugly and the " dirty " side of life. Since they will have to know it long enough when they do grow up, so it was reasoned, let's keep them happy and innocent as long as possible. An illusory world of morals, particularly sex morals, was therefore developed—with the unfortunate effects in neuroses, disorganized sex life, present marital incompatibility and unhappiness that we know about among the adults of to-day.

Present-day parents endeavour to avoid these pitfalls for their children by a franker attitude towards sex and all the catalogue of only slightly less dreadful " sins ".

Illusory worlds of " wickedness " and " purity " are no longer built up, but instead the child is given such information as he is able to assimilate from the time he begins asking questions. But even this does not end the matter. Many parents who have seen the necessity of admitting to theirchildren that they, too, are human, would still like to preserve the illusion that the world they live in is ideal. And so the process of building models of ideal behaviour with clay feet, which children will inevitably discover, still goes on. The more or less unconscious purpose to " protect " the child remains the same, differing only in form and content from that of our own parents. Two recent experiences may illustrate the old struggle to make the world seem better than it is.

An intelligent, informed mother of three children, ranging from eight to twelve, is aware of the particular clay feet she had to discover as she herself grew up, and with her own children she has carefully avoided undue concealment and misplaced emphasis along these particular lines. Yet she is distressed because it is " so difficult to keep the economic depression out of the home. One tries to, but it is almost impossible. My husband and I carefully avoid mentioning the subject at the table but guests are almost sure to bring it up. The children hear about it at school and on the street and come home troubled. One doesn't know what to do. It seems such an unsuitable topic for them."

A father and his two sons, aged ten and twelve, related with much excitement at the family dinner-table their experiences of the afternoon in Christmas shopping. After their adventures in the shops, the father had given each an extra sum of money and said that they would now walk about through the streets and give money to beggars. This had apparently been even more exciting than the shops. Each boy told of the beggar he had chosen and each felt that he had picked out the " best " beggar. Father, however, felt that his little old lady beggar was the best. All were happy in having shared.

The motive that lies behind both of these incidents would seem to be clear—to protect children from something, with the addition in the second instance of the further motive of teaching generosity to children. But is not the process the same as that which distorted our own point of view in childhood—the building up of an illusory world on the assumption that children should be kept " innocent " and not be allowed to know too much about some things ?

The depression may not be a suitable topic for family dinner-table discussion. One can quite understand the desire of the mother to make the dinner hour a cheerful one which all can enjoy. But " keeping the depression out of the home " implies much more. This mother is endeavouring to keep out the depression in just the same way that her mother endeavoured to keep out sex. The difference is only in what the two generations consider " suitable ". The mother of to-day desires to create a home for her children which will be full of happiness and to which in later troubled years they can look back with pleasure, even *sehnsucht*, and to her lovingly as the one who provided this for them. But is this wise ? Like her own mother she is creating an illusory world in which her children will be temporarily happy, but just as surely, too, she is digging a pit for them. And may they not come to look back upon her as she now looks back upon her mother, as one who indeed loved her children, and who did what she thought best for them—but with unhappy results?

Is there any reason why children should be " protected ", in this sense, from the facts about economics any more than from the facts about sex? These children may be living in a haven, thinking all other good people live in similar havens, but they are at best soon to be pitched out to discover that things in the outside world are quite otherwise. Would it not be better, and could it not be done without too great disturbance to the happiness and morale of the home, to discuss quite frankly with the children such elements in the depression and such facts about the present condition of the world as they are capable of understanding? Will they not look back to their home and to their parents with greater gratitude when they come to see how wisely they have been prepared to face the real facts, and how step by step they have been led into the larger world of reality so that they have been able to enter it with a minimum amount of shock?

The father, in the second incident, would also " protect " his two boys from knowing too much about present conditions. He teaches them sentiment but not a word of reality—beggars are unfortunate people to whom one must be generous and kind ; obviously, however, they live in one world and we in another. The fact that these boys must discover sooner or later is that we all live in the same world. Are boys of ten and twelve incapable of understanding some of the many reasons why these individuals are beggars while we are in a position to be " generous " to them?

There may perhaps be even more danger in the illusory world which is being built up for children to-day than in the illusory world of our childhood. Adolescents who have grown up in these modern " ideal " homes and " ideal " schools, where, instead of harshness, kindness, consideration and generosity have been shown them, where they have been treated as personalities, with deference and respect shown to their tastes and abilities, likes and dislikes, where everyone has appeared to be interested in them and to rejoice in the development of their talents and to desire their success, where they have learned that conscientious work brings respect and reward —these children, who have lived in this ideal world not knowing that there is another world outside, are finding themselves dismayed at the discovery of that world. It has come to them like a blow beneath the belt. The impact with the real world has sent some of them reeling and staggering and some to self-destruction.

It is probably not possible for children to avoid altogether the illusory worlds. Whether adults foster the illusions of childhood, children will more or less build them for themselves. Some disillusionment is bound to take place ; the discovery of some of the adult world's clay feet must probably remain one of the inevitable awakenings of youth. Our efforts as parents, however, should be to keep this from becoming devastating ; and it is clear that in order to do this it is necessary to be frank about more things than sex. Do we not make a mistake in " protecting " a child from anything ? Is there any safe principle other than the one we have adopted in the matter of sex education—that a child should be given such information as he is capable of understanding upon any subject at any time ?

## CHAPTER XIII

### ON THE RECOGNITION OF RUSSIA

THERE are excellent social, economic, and political reasons for the recognition of Russia, but since I am not expert in these fields I must leave their discussion to others. I wish to treat of the human side.

Why is it that so many sincere, earnest and high-minded people are so bitter against the Russians and the social experiment that is going on in Russia? It can only be because they do not know these Russians and do not understand what is actually taking place. We are inclined to think of the Russians as cruel, pagan, ruthless people, with ideals so different from our own that we cannot understand them. They seem more closely related to racketeers and gangsters than to ourselves. One finds them, however, not at all like racketeers but like our most earnest, sincere people. Their social interests and objects are the same as our own. Our aim is to build a society in which all can lead happy and worth-while lives. That is precisely what the Russians are endeavouring to do. There is absolutely no difference in aim although there is an important difference in emphasis. We say a happy and worth-while life for all, but in saying " all " we mean not necessarily now, as that would seem to be impossible, but eventually. The Russians place the emphasis upon the *all* and the *now*—and they do not believe it is impossible. Instead of the cruel, pagan, ruthless people we have been inclined to think them, one finds them with ideals quite like our own. They do not like the word " idealist " because they feel that idealists, such as ourselves, are likely to keep our ideals only in theory and not to put them into practice. They prefer to be realists which to them means taking ideals out of the realm of ideas and putting them practically to work. Their aims, however, are the same as our ideals. They have decided that these aims or ideals, our ideals, cannot be attained by our social method and have therefore changed the method. The result is that they are actually putting into practical effect the very fundamental Christian principles that we talk so much about and do so little about.

One often hears that in Russia there is no interest in the individual. This is a curious misconception, for the one thing that they are interested in is the welfare of the individual. The only reason that exists for the social organization in Russia is for the purpose of securing for each individual economic security, health, education, the development of whatever special artistic abilities the individual may have, provision for old age, and the like. Thought and energy are for the moment centred on economic development, but economics is a secondary interest, merely a means to an end. Much more so than here. The end, the real interest, is the welfare of the individual, every man, woman, and child, in the terms of health, education, and the development of talents. These to the Russians are vastly more important than economics ; economics exists only to provide these things.

How can we fear such a people ? What possible harm could they do us ? Why should we not learn from them ?

We have believed in our method of attaining these ideals, but our serious lack of success can cause us to doubt the correctness of our method.    Even in the best of times we have had great domestic unhappiness (as shown by the divorce rate), a tremendous amount of nervous and mental illness, much delinquency and poverty, and in bad times untold distress.    If from Russia we can learn to avoid these things—why not ?    If they have found a way that brings what we want, why refuse it ?    They are putting nothing over on us, so long as we are attaining only what we ourselves want, in the terms of our own social aims.

Fear has been expressed that with recognition of Russia, Russian ideas would become current in this country and disturb our ideals of the home, the church, morals, and the like.    But how can that really be ?    The ideals of the Russian home are not essentially different from ours.    If there is a difference between the American and the Russian home, it is this : we have not succeeded in making the average home a very happy or emotionally healthy place ; the Russian home is both healthy and happy.    No one, I believe, would insist that here we live really very significant spiritual lives : in Russia, on the other hand, there is a deep and rich spiritual life. What can we lose if we do nothing more than give up a shadow for a reality ?    The Russians have sometimes been thought to be lacking in morals.    They have one great moral principle—no one shall exploit another.    What could be finer, more fundamentally Christian, if you will, than that ?    Consider this principle—no one shall exploit another—in relation to business, to home life, to sex life, to school life, to every aspect of life that involves the relation of one individual to another.    How many problems that seem so complicated to us readjust themselves and become simpler when this one moral principle is applied ? Can we say they are without morals when this moral principle is the basis of their social structure ? Could this principle injure us ? It is at this point that ruthlessness comes into the Russian life. The Russian believes in this principle of no exploitation and will protect it and protect it ruthlessly if necessary. But isn't it a principle worth defending even with ruthlessness towards those who would violate it ?

Whatever the social, economic, or political reasons may be for recognizing Soviet Russia, my reason would be that the Russians are an earnest, sincere people, more deeply interested in the welfare of the average man and woman than any other nation so far as I know—if we are to judge by acts rather than by words ; a people whose ideals are the same as the best of ours, who differ from us only in the method by which these ideals are to be attained ; who with their method have had a far greater measure of success in attaining their ideals than have we and from whom, therefore, we might by closer relationship learn much that would be helpful to us in attaining our own highest ideals. We have more to gain by recognition than the Russians. From our recognition they will receive certain economic assistance, which they need, but from them we should receive spiritual, moral, and social values, which we need even more, and, if we wish to accept it, a technique for making these values effective in our own daily lives.

# CHAPTER XIV

## A CAT MAY LOOK AT A KING

THE world has been and still is in serious trouble. There is discussion of many things—monetary systems, economic laws, low and high tariffs, industrial relationships —so much discussion, in fact, and with so little agreement even among those expert in these matters, that most of us become confused. Talk of disarmament falls to the background and little is to be heard of pacifism. All that is left of these topics is some talk of co-operation and goodwill. It is significant that nothing is heard of love and brotherhood. We are so far from these things to-day that their discussion would seem a bit ridiculous. That we are discussing monetary systems and economic laws rather than love and brotherhood is encouraging in that it indicates that at least we are trying to deal with realities. That even these problems, in a sense, are not very real and that their discussion will not get us very far is at the moment of secondary importance. We are at least trying to be realistic.

Some of us working in other fields are not greatly impressed by the importance of what is going on. The very fact that such knowledge as we have is in other fields and that we do not understand monetary systems and can follow only slowly discussions of economic laws may be taken by some to explain why we attach so little importance to these things. We do not know enough about them, perhaps, even to know how important they are.    But we are probably not to be dismissed so easily. A cat may look at a king, and a psychiatrist may look at a statesmen.    Beneath the velvet breeches or the frock coat, both the cat and the psychiatrist find only the same human being with whom they have been familiar for a long time.    Velvet breeches, decorations, and frock coats are just a part of the picture so far as the cat and the psychiatrist are concerned and have no more importance to the cat and the psychiatrist than the less pleasant, noisy symptoms of some of the psychiatrist's other patients.    The belly of a queen is like any other belly to the surgeon who is determining where to make his incision to remove an infected appendix.    The loves and hates, emotions and sexual desires of the individual before the public eye, whether gangster, film star, or statesman, are just the same to the psychiatrist, except that they may be more confused than the emotional lives of lesser people.

To some of us it would seem that the sociologists and economists and the statesmen who put their decisions into codes and agreements are struggling through a period already passed by medicine.    To place the two in such juxtaposition is not as odd as it may seem at first.    There are certain laws that are common to all scientific fields. Sociology and economics have long been struggling to free themselves from the swamp of " philosophy ", in which they have been mired, and to become scientific. It is quite possible, therefore, for them to learn from the experience of any other scientific field which has made the same journey—and all have made it—no matter how different the content of the two fields.

Medicine was once in this same position—that of

freeing itself from " philosophy " and becoming scientific. At this period it began to " study " the conditions brought before it and to find remedies that would apply directly to the conditions found.   This was a step in the scientific direction, but only a step, for medicine had yet to learn that scientific methods could be applied either to the wrong thing or the right thing, and if to the wrong thing, while something was gained, not enough was gained to accomplish the purpose desired.   When the layman thinks of the great advances that have been made in the field of medicine, he thinks of the truly magnificent accomplishments in the field of surgery, or of the marvellous control of infectious disease, or of the advance in chemical knowledge which gives us such tools as insulin. These are indeed representative of the advance in medicine.   But only a physician knows, probably, that these are not the most significant things, but that the step that has been most significant and that has, indeed, made all these other things possible, is the step that led from focusing attention upon symptoms to the focusing of attention upon disease.

For a long period, not yet entirely passed, medicine's entire attention was upon the outstanding symptom.   A patient came with a headache, and the physician must find some way of relieving that headache.   A patient came with a pain in the chest or a pain in the abdomen and ways must be found to relieve these pains.   A patient's heart beat too fast.   A way must be found to reduce the heart's rapidity.   A patient had a fever and we must reduce that fever.   Proceeding scientifically, medicine was able to accomplish these things, but—the result ?   Relieved of his disagreeable symptom, the patient was grateful ; but often he became shortly afterwards violently ill and died—a disconcerting thing to do—and after so much work had been done on him. (Parenthetically it may be remarked, for it also has a bearing upon our present discussion, that another difficulty arose. At this point the physician, in order to increase his knowledge, was desirous of studying the body of his dead patient. But the body was too " sacred " to be submitted to such procedure. I am not talking about the Middle Ages but of a comparatively few years ago. To a not inconsiderable extent the view still obtains to-day and permission for autopsies that would yield knowledge of the greatest importance frequently cannot be obtained. The " sacredness " of the Middle Ages does continue even so late as to-day.)

Eventually, however, medicine did learn that a symptom is not a disease ; in fact, is not necessarily a destructive agent but a constructive agent in the sense that it represents an effort on the part of the body—often a too great effort and hence the individual's discomfort—to correct an unhealthy condition that does exist in the body ; that relieving a symptom, therefore, is not curing a disease but is, indeed, covering up the evidence of disease and leaving the disease to destroy the individual. The more successful the relief of the symptom itself, therefore, the greater the disservice and damage that has been done. Symptoms, medicine learned, are merely indicators that something is wrong somewhere. Although inconvenient they are not necessarily important in themselves and are to be largely ignored as objects of treatment while used as important direction-finders in tracking down the source of the trouble. The source of the trouble found and the condition corrected, the symptom will take care of itself. To the physician the headache may be considered as unimportant ; the important thing is the trouble in the kidney, or wherever else it may be. The pain in the side is unimportant—the inflammation of the appendix which is causing the pain is important. A rapid heart may not be important, but the resistance somewhere else in the circulatory system that makes necessary the increased beating of the heart is important. A fever may not be important but the infection somewhere in the body is important.  Any intelligent person can understand the importance of this re-orientation in the field of medicine, but its full significance is probably to be understood only by a medically trained person and an older person at that.  The younger men who have been taught this view from the beginning know no more about this transition than they know about taking a ride in the family carriage after Sunday dinner.

The sociologists and the economists would seem to be still in this period of symptom-treatment.  They do not believe this to be true and will deny it.  They will insist that their efforts are to get at social causes and to remedy these.  One does not have to be an expert in sociology or economics to point out that, in so far as they are looking for " social " causes for social ills, they are indeed enmeshing themselves in symptoms.  They are even farther away from the real cause of difficulty than was medicine in its " symptom " days.  It is a society that they are trying to heal, when it is people who are ill.  Society itself is but a symptom. Society may manifest itself in six or a dozen or more different kinds of headaches.  It may be inflation or deflation, nationalism or internationalism, war or pacifism. But whatever it is, so long as one treats it only socially, one is treating only headache, and, no matter how well

for a period the headache may be relieved, only a symptom has been relieved.   In fact it is as true here as in
medicine that the greater the success in the relief of the
symptom, the greater the disservice and the damage that
has been done.   For nothing at all has been done.
Although the patient no longer has a headache, the
situation remains the same, to grow progressively worse
until there is a violent illness.[1]

And here we may return to our second analogy with
medicine.   When medicine had reached this point, as
has been said, it was hindered in its progress by the view
that the body was too " sacred " to be violated by study
after death.   The sociologists and economists have come
to the point where further dissection becomes important,
and there is a tendency to block this dissection on the
same ground, that some things are too " sacred " to be
thus violated.   Bad men, their motives and compulsions,
may be examined, but good men with their motives and
compulsions are not to be examined.   Bad men should
probably be taken at their face value and be punished
for their badness—until recently this was the general
view and still is to a considerable extent ; but as there is
some evidence that bad men are not to be judged at
their face value, they may be examined.   But a good

[1] We may assume that in the exchange between men a
monetary system is necessary.   A good system will serve better
than a poor one.   We are justified, therefore, in devising the
best system possible.   But it is not money or a money system
that makes for us our real troubles—at most they make for
annoyance and inconvenience—but the use that man makes of
money.   A good system, as such, can be as badly used as a
poor system, and it is out of this use that real trouble comes.
Therefore it is men we must study in addition to or even
rather than monetary systems.   Did we understand men,
monetary systems would not so much matter.

man *is* to be taken at his face value.  Why not ?  Isn't he obviously good ?  What more can we ask ?  What could possibly be gained by examining him ?  And likewise " love " and " goodwill " and " the spirit of cooperation "—these are obviously good things that require no examination or any further understanding but emulation and encouragement.  Further dissection of these things will be accomplished only against heavy opposition.

Society is made of men.  The philosophy one holds in regard to the nature of man will determine his social attitude, his social thinking and his social planning.  What is the concept of man held to-day by sociologists and economists, by statesmen, industrialists, labour leaders, and by the great mass of people themselves ?  Where does this concept come from and what is its authority ?

The concept is not a modern product.  It comes from nothing that these people have themselves learned, or that others of their contemporaries have learned and passed over to them for their use, as in the case of the radio, the motor-car or the aeroplane, or the grapefruit.  It has no relationship to these things.  It is an ancient concept—more ancient than the views held in regard to the circulation of the blood at the time of Harvey, or of the nature of infectious disease at the time of Pasteur, or of the solar system at the time of Copernicus, or of the nature of gravity in the days of Newton—none of which views now affect the life or thinking of present-day sociologists, economists or statesmen—a concept more ancient than any of these, built up by wise men and thinkers in a period many hundred years before men knew even the simplest facts in regard to themselves or the world in which they lived. This concept still directs the thinking of sociologists, economists, and statesmen to-day as it did the statesmen in those early days, and not because it is any more true than were the concepts of that day in regard to the solar system and disease, but because it has never been replaced as have these other things by knowledge gained in the intervening years. A statesman broadcasts his views across the Atlantic. This is possible because the old views of physics and chemistry have been replaced by modern knowledge. But the views the statesman broadcasts are based upon a concept of the nature of man that in its fundamentals has not been changed by a thousand of years, and that has no more relationship to the realities that exist about him than if he read from a recently discovered papyrus on the diagnosis and treatment of disease.

In those days of wise men and thinkers—and they were indeed wise men and they could think—there was practically only one method available for thinking. Lacking facts, even an appreciation of facts, in our sense, or means of getting at facts, it was necessary to start with an assumption or a proposition in regard to the things about which they wished to think. The proposition once stated was then assumed to be true. And starting from this assumption and reasoning logically, they could reach and claim true whatever conclusions they did reach by this process—men, nature, the world, and the heavens could be explained and were explained, and all intelligently, in the sense of logically, done. That none of it happens to be true is indeed important to us, but in no way detracts from the intelligent and logical feat of these men.

From the explanations so arrived at came the philosophies in regard to men and life that determine men's social planning, not only then *but now*.

Side by side with this form of reasoning—deductive reasoning—but almost unnoticed, was another method of arriving at explanations—inductive reasoning. Deductive reasoning ruled the world. Inductive reasoning was about as important then as communistic reasoning is to-day to capitalistic reasoning in the field of social economy— to be tolerated as long as not too bothersome, to be attacked and destroyed (driven underground) if too bothersome.

Inductive reasoning starts with an observation. An object is to be explained. It is observed in as many aspects as possible—no assumptions are made in regard to it. The first observations are followed by second observations in order to test the accuracy of the first. Experiments are devised by which to test again the " facts " that seem to have been determined in order to prove whether they are true or not true. Instruments and methods are devised to make even finer and more accurate the observations. Facts once obtained, working hypotheses and theories may be constructed from them in order to advance toward additional facts. But the object always is not to prove that a certain hypothesis or theory is true but to obtain facts that will establish either that it is true or is not true. Hypotheses and theories are not sacred ; they can be altered or discarded at any time—only facts are important. And no matter how far hypotheses or theories may be extended the method rests upon observations and a checking and rechecking of the observations and of the facts apparently obtained. Even " facts " are not sacred and can be discarded whenever new methods or instruments show them not to be facts.

By this method, of so little consequence in the days
when deductive reasoning ruled the world, has come
our modern world—our modern world not only of things
such as radios, aeroplanes and electrical refrigerators—
but our modern world of ideas in regard to the world
in which we live, the sky above us and the sea beneath
us, so entirely different from the explanations devised
by the deductive thinkers of earlier times. *This is true
in every field in which we move except one*—our ideas in
regard to man and the relationship of man to man.  In
regard to the nature of man these early ideas remain,
and again, not because the many hundreds of years that
have passed have proven them to be true, but merely
because these ideas have never been replaced in the minds
of men generally, including sociologists, economists and
statesmen, with knowledge of man obtained during this
period.

To be sure some of our ideas in regard to man have
been changed. We may no longer believe that God
made woman from a rib taken from Adam (although
many sociologists, economists, and statesmen give allegi-
ance to a church that does hold this to be true).  We have
changed our notions in regard to man's history, anatomy
and physiology ; but we have not changed our notions
in regard to man's fundamental nature, although the
imaginary man built up by the early philosophers bears
no more relationship to real man than the real world
bears to the fiction world of the early philosophers.  And
yet it is *this concept* of man that determines the thinking
of sociologists, economists and statesmen to-day as they
work with men and plan for men.  It is as impossible to
make progress in our dealing with each other on the
basis of these concepts as it would be did we try to repair

a wireless-set or motor-car using the conception of physics that existed at the time our present concept of man was developed.    Consequently we can advance surefootedly and successfully in any field of activity, with such success, in fact, as to be embarrassing to us, except in the field of human relationships.

Our human relationships confuse us.    Why this is so is not puzzling.    Men make it a puzzle, but only because they examine the phenomena with the light of the taper-concept they hold in their hands.    Our relationships, one to another, are dictated by our codes of ethics, of morals, our religion, our social system and our form of government.    These present-day systems of ethics, morals, religion, and the social system and government that have grown out of them, are the only remaining edifices of a world, a method of arriving at explanations and a system of ideas that is utterly dead.[1]

Our confusion will not be less until we become as realistic in regard to man as we are in regard to man's world and until the ethics, morals, religion, built up on a fiction of man, are replaced by an ethics, system of morals, government, even, perhaps, religion based upon facts in regard to man.[2]

What is this fiction-man with which we deal ?    He has so many aspects that it would be impossible to deal with them all here.    With one important aspect, however, we can at least deal in part.

[1] For a discussion of this in reference to a lesser matter, the conflict between law and medicine (psychiatry), see the chapter " What Has Been Done to Prevent Delinquency ? " in *Adolescence : Studies in Mental Hygiene*, by Frankwood E. Williams, M.D.

[2] See also Chapter VII, " Youth and the Present-Day World ".

It is held that man is part " good " and part " bad ".
The " good " was and still is somehow related to an
assumed " god " and the " bad " to the " devil ".
" God " still remains with us but the " devil " has more
or less dropped out.   Love became representative of the
" good " and hate or aggression against others representative of the " bad ".   As to love others was obviously " good ", while to be aggressive against them
was obviously " bad ", the obligation was laid upon
us to love and not to hate.   It was also thought, and
is still thought to-day, that decisions in these matters
man could make with his intellect and enforce by his
will.   It then becomes a moral duty to love and not to
hate.   It was thought—and it is still thought to-day—
that through the use of intellect and will one could fill
his life with love and thereby crush out tendencies to
hate or to be aggressive, all of which is as far from the
truth as motor transportation is from camel-back.

Modern investigation shows that what we are dealing
with is energy ; that this energy works itself out in accordance with certain fundamental needs of man and certain
fundamental laws ;   that over the play of forces that
determines in any given instance how this energy shall
be worked out man has about as much control as he has
over his intestinal tract or circulation ; that he can indeed
control to a certain extent the surface manifestations of
this energy, but that this changes nothing fundamental
at all, except as his effort adds to the play of forces at
work and only to his increased confusion ; that useful
as his intellect is in adding two and two until he eventually
builds a bridge, its greatest use to him, in determining
the play of these forces, is as a rationalizing agent to
explain after the event what it was all about and why he

took the course he did. The most distinguished statesman or the most eminent churchman, when it comes to
the play of these forces, has about as much control over
the situation as a child driving a horse holding the tail
of the reins behind the hands of a grown-up. Just so is
it to-day. But this is largely because the statesman and
churchman and man in the street misunderstand the
forces. This energy, as other energy, electrical, lightning
—and not just by analogy—if understood can be utilized.

Love will not crush out hate in any individual, no matter
how much it may appear to do so. It is this appearance
of things that we have taken too seriously and that deceives
us. It does not take a great deal of investigation to show
that the face value of ourselves, of others or of human
relations in general is one hundred per cent untrustworthy.
We really know this quite well enough. It may take
scientific investigation to prove it, but it does not take
scientific investigation to make us aware of it. Literature
has always been full of it. Events of daily life repeatedly
make us aware of it. But so imbedded within us is our
philosophy of human beings that we can discount literature as just literature, and the unpleasant events of daily
life, even the experience of the World War, with our most
gentle " good people " suddenly turning blood-thirsty,
we can hold to be only exceptions. We have indeed a
folk expression, " a wolf in sheep's clothing ". We know
there are wolves in sheep's clothing, but again we hold
these to be only exceptions. What we have to come to
see is that we are all wolves in sheep's clothing with not
one exception, from the head of the church to the gangster.

Hate and aggression being outlawed, but by no means
done away with, must be provided for, and in order to
maintain the fiction our philosophy represents, must be

provided for in some way that we are not aware of. The great mass outlet that has been found is economic exploitation. Here under the highly moral terms of courage, initiative, ambition, social service, liberty, individualism, we hide and make legal and moral the very aggression we have before condemned. This deceptive outlet proves a boomerang which returns to smite us each time as we are in the very act of congratulating ourselves on the development of civilization to the point where certain things " can never happen again ". And each time we are dumbfounded ; but there is nothing inexplicable about it. That things do " happen again " is logical and quite to be expected and could have been prophesied two thousand years ago if men had had the knowledge of men that we have to-day.

Hate unsuccessfully overlaid by love, outlawed but not destroyed, backs up until men are gorged with it. Economic exploitation, the devious outlet, not only fails as a drainage system but actually increases by its own activities (legal and moral though they may be) the quota of hatred, and instead of the civilized peace and goodwill towards which we thought we were working, we find ourselves in a position where even co-operation can only be wistfully talked about. Our effort has been to teach men how to love, or, at least, the necessity of loving. The result is a " civilized " individual who has learned the forms, the vocabulary and the gestures of love, but who continues to hate to the point of destruction of himself and others.

We need not be so concerned about love. Love is a fundamental need of men, and men will find love without direction. What we need to do is to teach men to hate, but to hate—extraordinary as it would seem—constructively, which would mean to hate openly and above board, without any sense of guilt, but to hate first—extraordinary as it would seem—with discrimination until the social house is somewhat in order (for it will take force to put the house in order) and then to utilize the energy now manifested in hate in socially constructive ways. The way out is not through hating less but through hating more. We have no choice. The hate is here and at flood tide. The most damaging thing that could happen would be for the moment successfully to overlay this hate with love. It would but dam things up temporarily to burst forth eventually with devastating force. Our choice is between misunderstanding completely with what we have to deal and permitting hate to break through our misdirected efforts at restraint into senseless, socially destructive national wars, and, understanding with what we have to deal—seeing it in all its aspects, stripping off all the moral, ethical and legal cover words—to direct hate towards the destruction of those things and systems, which means, of course, eventually the people representing and defending those things and systems, that are in themselves socially destructive. Can this be done ? At least one great nation of one hundred and sixty million people, covering a sixth of the earth's surface, has done it.

We have all with growing admiration watched President Roosevelt as he and his advisers have courageously taken hold of the problems that faced him and us all as he assumed office. Frightened by the depth to which we had fallen, all were ready to co-operate and, with surprisingly slight opposition, powers were granted to the President which if ever called into force would represent a revolution in our economic life. The President's programme, in brief, is to stop the grossest exploitation, most of which previously had been legal, moral and right, and to " distribute wealth more evenly by humanitarian consideration ", " to turn the results of common effort toward more general benefits—enlarged incomes for common people, greater leisure, security from risks ". The principle of exploitation remains, but through a more careful regulation it is to be made a better and more comfortable form of exploitation. " Rugged individualism" is banned, but individualism as an " initiating " and " stimulating " force is to remain, but more carefully policed. The country as a whole, even including those who, formerly holding high place, had to humiliate themselves by confessing publicly what they had been doing, were ready to co-operate.

It is interesting and instructive to note what happened not with the return of " prosperity " but at the first faint sign of a change for the better—hesitation, and then a definite holding back by those who had been so ready and eager to co-operate ; only threats, definite and direct, reinspired the spirit of co-operation in the recalcitrant.

Nothing is changed. Men are the same after these powers have been given to the President as they were before they were given to him. It may be replied that men may not be different but they must at least act as though they were. That is the pit into which we continue to fall—we must at least act as though we were different from what we are. Our conduct becomes changed in its externals, but remains always the same in its fundamentals ; and the real result is no change at all. We remain precisely what we were before and we do precisely what we did before, except in a different way and with mounting confusion to ourselves as we weave these intricately patterned webs about ourselves.

Should the President use to the full every power that
has been granted to him—assuming that he would have
the courage to do this, and so far we have no reason to
question his courage, except that his responsibility would
test the courage of any man, and assuming that he would
actually be permitted to utilize these powers, which is
indeed an open question—our economic life would be
revolutionized in a way that was never dreamed of as
possible even a month before he took office.   But actually
it would make little difference.   The President would be
attempting, and in the face of our very recent experience
with prohibition, the constitutional amendment for which
it was a part of his programme to repeal, to make men good
by law.   The President and his party were right in saying
in regard to prohibition that men could not be made good
by law.   If men cannot be made by law to give up what
is nothing more to them than an escape from the sharp
edges of living, why should we think that men can be
forced by law to give up the most powerful force that
exists within them ?

During the darkest days of the " depression ", when
men's minds searched in all directions for ways out, there
was a good deal of talk by many who believed that they
had ceased being just " liberal " and had actually become
" radical ", that the principle of co-operative economic life
was essentially sound, but that it would not be possible
to accept for use here the Russian model, for the reason
that Americans are very different from Russians, and
American life very different from anything ever known to
the Russians ;   that a form of planned and co-operative
economic life must be worked out that would be in accordance with our life and traditions.   We shall now have
something of an opportunity to see.   Mr. Roosevelt's plan

is a step and can be a very large step in this direction. But one does not hesitate to prophesy in regard to it, or even in regard to a still larger step of the same kind. It may succeed—perhaps even amazingly—but the success can only be temporary. Revolutionary as Mr. Roosevelt's programme can be, it is mechanical only. It is founded on the same principles as what went before. It represents no change in philosophy, no change in social aim in consequence of a change in philosophy. " Larger incomes for common people ", " wealth more evenly distributed ", as here enunciated, is not a change in social aim. This carries with it all that has been fundamentally vicious and destructive. Only the rules, not the game, are changed. The " common man " must, if he is to respect himself and have the respect of others, increase this common minimum wealth to something much more. And he can do so if he will but be a bit more aggressive than his fellows ; and a bit more will get him a bit farther.

There can be no permanent change until our philosophy of life and of man has been changed. So long as our thinking and planning are determined by a concept and a philosophy that deal with a fiction-man and ignore actual man, it matters little what we do. If an object lies north it matters little how well or how earnestly we argue whether we should turn east or west. The greatest misconception that people have in the United States of what is going on in Russia is that the important thing going on in Russia is economic planning. Bulking large as it does and having its own importance, it is, as a matter of fact, but an incident in something of much greater importance. The most important thing about Russia is that this fiction-straw-man of history, built up out of men's minds, has been completely destroyed and with him the philosophy that bore him, and men are dealing with men as men in accordance only with what knowledge they can have in regard to men.

The greatest evil in the world to-day is the keeping up of the fiction in regard to man. The activities of a racketeer are inconsequential as compared to the activities of good men who continue to teach these fictions. There must come a revaluation of things in the light of modern knowledge and this may well begin with a study of what is " good ". Educators have been slow in learning, but they have in large part now learned, that it is the " good " child, the child who never gives anyone any difficulty, who always has his lessons and who is always well behaved, who is often in greater psychic danger and more greatly in need of help than the boisterous, troublesome child upon whom they had formerly been accustomed to centre their attention as a " problem child ". In our adult world we have not yet begun to learn this. But we shall become increasingly more suspicious of " good " people and come to examine them more closely. We have not been brought to our present pass by " bad " people but by " good " people.

Until our concept of man is brought into accord with the known facts in regard to man, and an ethics, and a system of morals and government and philosophy of life has been constructed from these facts, our best brains can do no more than to attempt to devise and cure mere symptoms that arise from time to time. Sociology must learn eventually, as has medicine, that this ends only in disaster ; that, indeed, as has been said, the more success-ful the apparent cure, the greater the damage that has been done. Wise sociologists, like wise physicians, will come to ignore symptoms, more or less, as objects of treatment and will use them as indicators of and assistants in locating the disease against which curative forces are to be mobilized. Although not a sociologist, one does not hesitate in the present instance to make a diagnosis —for the difficulties in which the world finds itself at the present time are " sociological " only in a word sense ; they are really just human problems, not nearly so mysteriously complex as they are made out to be, problems of which one who deals with human problems can have some understanding—to make a diagnosis. The disease from which we suffer is insecurity, caused by exploitation, on the principle of which our social structure has been erected, which principle has been used in forming this structure because of a misconception, misunderstanding and therefore mishandling of the problem of hate. In curing this disease there would appear to be two points of attack. In reality there is but one. If our difficulties are due to exploitation, then it would seem reasonable to attack exploitation. This in a " reasonable " way is President Roosevelt's New Deal. The final attack will be upon exploitation, but in a vigorous, ruthless, wholly unreasonable way, as we conceive this term now. But while it is true that our immediate difficulties are caused by exploitation, exploitation is itself a result and not a primary cause. Our attack must be upon the archaic concept of hate now generally held. It is this concept, which of course involves the whole concept of man, that is the vitiating agent that permits the exploitation that in the end brings such mass insecurity that our structure collapses.

Hate can be treated neither as a poor relation and a nuisance to be ignored as much as possible, nor as a mere incident in the life of man to be deplored with a few unctuous words.  Neither the concept that man is essentially good although he has a bad streak in him which requires a certain amount of policing, nor the concept that man is essentially bad and must be redeemed, is in accordance with the facts.  Hate is as much a part of man as love.  The duality must be dealt with openly as such and provision made for direct and adequate expression of the energies tied up in each of these aspects.

For the moment we are faced with a pathological situation due to the amount of hate that has been generated and damned up in the world.  We have, therefore, two problems rather than one to deal with : (1) what to do with this hate already generated ; (2) how to plan eventually for the utilization of man's aggression.

As to the first problem there is but one solution—to use a medical term—drainage.  When through a broken appendix an abdomen is filled with poisonous pus, the surgeon does not, with a shocked and sanctimonious air, pull the bed-clothes up quickly to hide the disgraceful situation, urging the patient and his family not to say a word about it, but to think happy thoughts of the beauty of the world, the sweetness of children, the sacrificing love of mothers, the great goodness of God who loves and looks after us all, even sparrows, with such a great love we cannot even understand it.  Rather he jerks off the bed-clothes, as it were, and with as little loss of time as possible opens the abdomen and puts in a drain by which the poisons may be carried away and the body given an opportunity to recover itself to the point where something more can be done.  The question is not whether we can keep men's hate from spilling over— the time for that is past ; in fact, there never was a time for it ; it has always been an unreal question—but whether

it shall spill over blindly and destructively as in nationalistic wars, or whether, as it comes, it can be utilized
in socially constructive ways.  It is subject to direction,
as we have seen in nationalistic wars.  Nationalistic wars
leave things as they were except for geographical boun-
daries.  Or it can be directed into revolution as we have
seen in Germany.  But such revolutions leave things
as they were except for a change in personnel.  Our
choice is as between these two and a third which would
utilize this hatred in the destruction of exploitation,
actually and in principle, and the destruction of all those
agencies that maintain and continue to promulgate the
concept and philosophy of a fiction-man.[1]

The immediate pathological condition having been
alleviated, and with it those elements that made the
situation a vicious circle destroyed, we are faced with the

---

[1] The mere statement of this disturbs us.  It disturbs us so
deeply that the impulse comes not only to deny it angrily but
to fight against any such idea.  Why does it disturb us ?—for
a reason that lies very close to us.  It negates our own lives
or what we had come to think of as the best part of our lives.
Still more, for we may not consider that our own lives are very
important, it negates and makes useless the lives of those whom
we have loved, admired and followed.  But this is not true.
It does not negate and make useless these lives.  These people
have lived bravely, and lived intelligently and have worked
devotedly.  It is for this we love and admire them, not for
any special accomplishment.  What has appeared as an accomplishment now turns out not to have the value it was thought
to have had—in other words a negative experiment.  But a
scientist is not to be judged by his negative results, and neither
is a human being.  An experiment that has ended in a negative
result has not been a useless experiment.  It takes its place
definitely and usefully in the accumulation of knowledge.
And so do the lives and the work of social leaders.  Their
lives and their work have been necessary and useful in the
total experience of living.  But even though this were not so
the fact would remain the same.

immediate practical problem of building a social structure upon a non-exploiting basis and the further problem of utilizing the energy of man's aggression in socially constructive ways. This latter problem resolves itself into two parts : (1) that of keeping at a healthy level the amount of aggression within man ; (2) that of utilizing that energy.

The solution of these problems will come through further experimentation. By dealing with man on a realistic basis we can approach these experiments with considerable confidence. It is already to be observed how extraordinary is the effect on human beings of a non-exploiting society guided by a realistic philosophy of life and of men. Values stand out honestly and clearly and without neurotic confusion. There is not a department of life, public life, family life, sex life, work life, spiritual life, that is not blown through and revivified and made vital as by a fresh breeze through a sick-room. The effect is noticeable even upon older people warped, twisted and scarred by the road along which they have come. The result in child life, mentally, physically and spiritually healthy, makes us pause in amazement. It is this that may give us any courage we may need. Developing in our neurotic world where everything must be different from what it actually is, where the left hand must never know what the constantly busy right hand is doing, in a world as much on its psychological head as it can be, there is no possible way for children to develop without carrying with them an accumulation of aggression that in the end becomes socially destructive. On the other hand, children with certainly no better potentialities developing in a rational and realistic environment do not, so far as at the moment can be seen, carry along any more accumulation of aggression than would seem could be handled by an adult through the avenues of work, sexual activity and avocation. This remains yet to be seen, but we can at least be sure that the movement is in the right direction and any degree of failure means merely further study of the situation. The end in terms of adulthood cannot be worse ; it can only be better.    Doubt at the moment can be entertained only in regard to the amount of the betterment.

# CHAPTER XV

## PROSPECTS : RUSSIAN AND AMERICAN YOUTH

RETURNING from Russia it is impossible not to make comparisons. These arise in one's mind involuntarily and certainly are not always unfavourable to us. It *is* comfortable to be comfortable, that cannot be denied, and one sinks back gratefully into such comforts as one has built around oneself. It *is* pleasant to have agreeable rooms, a variety of things to eat in accordance with one's appetite, to find in the shops a selection of articles one may need for dress or toilet or house, to be able to move rapidly from one part of the city to another. But as one sinks back with satisfaction into these physical comforts one's mind goes on turning and turning. After all, the Russians do not deny the satisfaction and desirability of these comforts. They would merely say, " Indeed you have them. But at what a price ! We expect to have them, too, or at least such of them as are really desirable ; but at a very much less price. They are not worth what you pay, what you must pay." And they are, of course, right. Any one of us who lives by the work he does pays far too much in work-energy for such comforts as he has ; and many, of course, who expend even more energy and time and, often, in more socially constructive ways, have even fewer comforts.

But the thing that impresses one most, on returning, is the change in oneself or, at least, in one's relation to the

whirl of life about one. One was once a part of it, but
now it seems a bit alien and queer. There is so much
talk and talk, a seeming endless flow of words; it takes
so many words to say such simple things and a thing
once said in all its " complexity " must be repeated again
and finally all summed up once more. There are so many
committees and boards and organizations and meetings
and letters and telegrams and telephone calls and it all
seems urgent and important and yet, somehow, it doesn't
seem very important at all. It seems mostly noise and
nervousness. Meetings struggle through hours and in
the end are about where they were in the beginning and
at that they have only ratified once more, in a somewhat
different vocabulary, the platitudes that have been ratified
at hundreds of previous meetings since the time of our
parents and grandparents. So much that one sees going
on about seems so useless, such a running about, so much
up hill and down dale, such fuss and feathers.

One becomes suspicious of oneself. Why this distaste
for things ? Why this feeling of the futility of all this
activity ? Why these negative feelings and thoughts that
keep rising in spite of oneself ? Is it merely disgruntle-
ment at the loss of holiday freedom and a distaste for
getting back to work ? Is it an arrogance that comes to
cover disappointment at lack of personal achievement ;
a superiority to cover an inability to grapple successfully
with things ? Is it age that takes away one's interest and
enthusiasm ?

One realizes that it can be all of these things or any
one or combination of them ; but one is not satisfied
with this explanation, for, deep within, one is aware of
a more vital interest in things than ever before, and of
less personal feeling in relation to things, less ambition,

less need for recognition or approval, greater satisfaction
in the circle of one's personal life. It is not so much
that one renounces these former interests and activities ;
it is simply that they seem to have dropped out through
loss of meaning and significance. . . . Gradually it
becomes clearer . . . a contrast begins to formulate itself
in one's mind between the simplicity and directness
of thinking, activity and relationships in Russia and
what now seems the curious complexity of these things
here.

It has not always seemed curious. Complexity was just
a part of things. Into all thinking, activity, relationship
must come many things for consideration and complexity
cannot be avoided. In any decision many things must
be balanced against each other. This is as obvious as
wind and rain and one has gone through with it, with
weariness sometimes, but without great complaint.

Now, however, it is disturbing and confusing. One
draws back from it as from some unknown danger, something unhealthy, something to keep away from, not to
get mixed up in. One watches one's friends and col-
leagues at their busy activities, talking, conferring, writing,
making programmes, modifying programmes, making
them all over again, forming more committees, talking
and making still more programmes, calling conferences,
all very serious and earnest, smiling and co-operative—
in fact, the aim in all this making and unmaking seems
to be pleasant. One reads what the leading ministers
have to say ; one notes what the university presidents are
saying to their students, the advice the economists and
sociologists are giving, the bankers, the industrialists and
labour leaders, the mayors and governors, the discussions
in the Congress and the legislatures, the judgments from

the bench.   All this goes whirling by and then gradually something familiar begins to work out of it all.   Where have I seen this before ?   What is this like ? . . .   It is just plain neurotic conduct.   Nothing is simple.   What is really simple is made complex, what is a bit complex is made more complex, really complex things are brought to utter confusion.   Everywhere furious grappling with shadows, never with substance.   Avoiding realities almost in panic and struggling furiously with unrealities—and with such a clatter of explaining and proving, proving and explaining.   And always so convinced of the proof and explanation and yet really never convinced.   Making plans but only for the purpose of making other plans that will defeat the first plans, for the object really, strange as it may seem, is not to get on but to keep defeated.   The need is not for success but for failure.   There must always be a cry for peace and quietude but there must be no peace and quietude : life is in the eternal, painful struggle.   And, in the last analysis, all getting back to the neurotic base of eating one's cake and having it too.   The talking, the explaining, the proving, the if- and the and- and the buting, and the complexities all swing from this rather than from the intricacies of things themselves.

Things are really not so complex—the relation of a man to a woman, a child to its parents, of one worker to another worker, of an individual to the group, of one group to another group.   One has seen these things treated simply and directly, with the simple directness of common sense, the open-eyed directness of a child, and instead of this treatment ending in confusion and absurdity one has seen it result in the beginning of a new humanity and civilization, a step as great in the matter

of human relations as the step from alchemy to science
in the field of mechanics.

Nineteen hundred and some years ago we made a
detour and we are still struggling in that by-path.  It has
been considered that a step in civilization was taken
when the Christians overcame the pagans of the Harz
Mountains and those of the rest of the western world.
It will come to be seen that this was no advance, merely
the substitution of one mythology for another, a change
only in outer form, in nothing fundamental, and that
such advance as has been made in the physical comforts
of living has been made in spite of and not because of
this new philosophy and that likewise any human advance
will be made in spite of and not because of this philosophy.  It will be seen that these nineteen hundred
years have been but a struggle through a morass of false
issues, with the learned men discussing these false issues
as earnestly and as effectively as those of the Middle
Ages discussed the question as to the number of angels
that could stand on the point of a needle.  And in the
end it comes to nothing more than the commonplace—
How can I eat my cake and have it, too ?  From this the
complexity, for this the committees, the organizations,
the meetings, the conferences, the plans and counter-
plans, the books and speeches and sermons and commencement addresses, the whir of typewriters, the click
of telegraph instruments, the ring of telephones, the
coming and going.  One nation alone has had the insight
and courage to close this detour, to destroy it and to
push its way through to ground upon which it can build
continuously and constructively.

No.  After the first confusion of feeling strange in a
once familiar world one regains one's assurance and

does not accept as the full explanation that one is himself at fault. No, there was once a similar situation when as a young medical officer one sat in one's room in the mental hospital. Here was a table, there a chair, here a pencil, there a pen. These things were all quite simple and real. But behind and all round were corridor upon corridor where chairs and tables, pens and pencils were not chairs and tables, pens and pencils. Napoleons marched their armies about, great actors promenaded with awesome dignity, politicians harangued the populace, millionaires counted their money, inventors with carefully placed slips of paper controlled the weather throughout the world, John the Baptists exhorted and Jesus Christs stood or knelt in corners overcome with grief at a world that misunderstood them and would not be saved. We called those people crazy, but their thoughts were so often like ours and our thoughts were so often like theirs that we could wonder who indeed was crazy. At least might we not be crazy, too? But clinging to chairs and pencils and tables as realities we decided not, and sought ways of bringing them to see that a chair was a chair and a table a table. So, too, now will we stick to certain simplicities and let others find such satisfaction as they may in their complexities.

But this concerns one's own adult world and while it has importance it isn't nearly so important as comparisons elsewhere. As one faces daily American youths, puzzled as to their present and future, a comparison with Russian youths and of the outlook for these two will formulate itself.

What is the prospect for the average American and Russian youth? What would be an " average " life experience in either case it would be impossible to know, but it is not impossible to formulate a picture of what is happening and what will happen in the life of each that will be recognized as generally true—at least true for a very large number. A comparison must in each instance begin with the parents and the influences that have been at work in the formation of the character and personality of these youths.

### PARENTS : AMERICAN

Probably about twenty-five years of age. Both " well ", in the sense of not sick, but neither up to their physical maximum. The father, if in the city, a bit below weight ; the mother soft through keeping her weight down by unwise dieting rather than by exercise.

They are in love. They have wanted to marry for some time but have been unable to do so for financial reasons. Before marriage the wife held a clerical position and enjoyed the work and the life of downtown and the office. Or she may still hold her position, as the combined salaries may be necessary for the maintenance of the home. He has a white-collar position, which, after several years, now pays enough, with the most careful planning, to maintain a modest apartment an hour or an hour and a half's ride from the office, or his salary may be insufficient to cover these minimum expenses and the salary of the wife must help out, or help must come from one or both of the families.

Marriage has been a ponderous decision for both, not only because of lack of funds, but because of its serious implication—a final, perhaps fatal, decision ; once made, nothing can be done about it, in many instances, and if anything is done about it, it can only be done through much suffering and humiliation and bitterness. Both have wondered what it is " to be in love ", whether they are in love, but both have decided that they are and for ever, and both have entered upon the undertaking with hope, some courage and determination to make life as pleasant for one another as possible—but with doubts which will take many forms but most likely a repeated searching, silently on the part of both, to see if month by month they are still in love, and near panic, particularly on the part of the wife, if any evidence appears that the love may be a little less. For she has tied her fortunes to this man. What happens to him, either emotionally within himself, or in success or failure in the outside world, is of vital importance to her. No matter what her abilities are, nor how well she may have been able to manage for herself, she is now dependent upon the fortunes of this man and will become increasingly so. She is aware of it, regardless of how bravely she may talk of her former training to fall back upon ; and with the awareness there is anxiety.

They both want children—but not now. They can't possibly afford a child now, they fairly shudder to think of the expense. Neither has anything like an adequate knowledge of sex. Both may have had sexual experience, but if so it is likely to have been a guilty, unpleasant, cheap and degrading rather than revealing experience. The likelihood is that neither has had sex experience and that they are now utterly awkward in their approach to one another. Their bodies are strange to each other. What was " wrong " the day before marriage has not become " right " the day after, nor six months later, nor probably ever will. Although they will eventually accept it, sex will never become a comfortable subject for them to the end of their days. What was psychologically built

up in them to make it " wrong " will be more enduring
and determining than any latter experience.

But not inhibitions alone keep them from discovering
each other completely, but also lack of knowledge of procedure.  (A man, whose duty it was to instruct the young
in morals and their parents in the right way of living,
wonders, after four years of marriage, why he and his
wife are on the edge of nervous illness through lack of
satisfactory sexual relations when they have followed
faithfully the instruction of animals and barn-yard fowl
that sexual approach is from the rear.  An exaggerated
case, to be sure, but more nearly representative of the
knowledge, at the time of marriage, of the parents of
present-day youths than freedom and release in sexual
relations.)  Through a year of marriage the wife has
grown increasingly distraught through lack of satisfaction and whatever dislike of sex she brought to the marriage is now increased and she accepts intercourse only
as a wholly unpleasant duty or avoids it.  The husband
is unhappy at his apparent inability to bring adequate
satisfaction to his wife and at the same time is resentful
of her attitude which spoils satisfaction for himself.
Tension develops between them.

And always there is the spectre of pregnancy.  If per-
chance they have found a satisfactory relationship, they
are never free to give themselves unreservedly to it.
Every moment they must be self-conscious.  Every
moment alert.  If guilt has been overcome, fear has
become the predominant emotion of their relationship.
And not only fear of the moment but a fear from day to
day.  Every menstrual period is watched with anxiety.
And if the menstrual period is delayed for a few days
there is a sickening anxiety that at times may become

panic so that nothing else can be thought of. Month
after month does slip by but eventually the fatal month
comes—and there can be no question ; the wife is pregnant. There are tears and anger, probably recriminations,
but mostly despair as to how on their slim funds they are
going to manage. If she has been working she will
sooner or later resign her position, cutting the family
income almost, if not quite, by half. She may or may
not receive pre-natal care, depending upon what the
facilities may be, what she may more or less accidentally
know of these facilities, what the costs may be if it is
through private arrangement.

### PARENTS : UNION OF SOVIET SOCIALIST REPUBLICS [1]

The parents will be in the early twenties, she perhaps
twenty, he twenty-two, or she eighteen and he twenty or
twenty-two. Both are robust in health. She has little
or no excess fat but is well developed, well muscled and
strong. They are in love and quite delightfully so, but
neither is under the delusion that the other is Heaven-
sent and the only person that he or she could ever consent to marry. They may have been in love before, they
realize they may be in love again, but that causes no
dismay. They are thoroughly serious in their present
desire to marry and look forward expectantly to a happy
life together. Marriage is not a matter of breath-taking
solemnity for either of them. In love as they are, and
with the best of intentions, they realize that it may turn
out that they are not suited to each other. But this does

[1] For a more extended discussion see Chapter II, " The
Psychologic Bases of Soviet Success " (pp. 7–28), in *The New
Russia ; Between the First and Second Five-Year Plans*, edited
by Jerome Davis.

not disturb them.  A divorce can be obtained at any time in ten minutes by either of them—without any grounds being given and without any unnecessary bitterness or humiliation.  If there are children they will be provided for until they are eighteen.  There will be pain in such separation, but with maintenance of self-respect and far less pain than living for years with one whom one has ceased to love or who has ceased to love in return.

But they are not thinking now of divorce but of marriage and of founding a home and this they can freely and happily do for the very reason that marriage places no halters about their necks.  The marriage ceremony will be brief, consisting merely in the registering of their names and other data in regard to themselves at the local marriage bureau.  Their greatest difficulty will be in finding a suitable place in which to live.  They have a legal right to a certain amount of space and this they will obtain as soon as, in the housing shortage, it becomes available.  It may be ready for them now.  If not they will probably double up with someone else or occupy the space one or the other has occupied before.

Both are working, and at comparable wages, and neither is economically dependent upon the other.  The wife's fate is not tied irrevocably to the fate of the husband.  Together or alone they have adequate funds for present needs and there need be no looking forward to a possible " rainy day "—accident, sickness, child-birth, holiday, education, total or partial incapacity, old age are provided for.  Their energy need not be wasted in anxiety over the future or in disappointment and irritation over present skimping and denials.  If they have to deny themselves, and they will, it will not be for the purpose of saving but because the market does not contain at the

moment the thing they want.   This may be a disappointment but not serious, for from past experience they are
quite confident that eventually the market will have what
they want.   There will be no savings bank, no counting
of pennies, no recrimination about expense, no denial
of this or that, except for an immediate purpose, for by
the end of the month all money will be expended, not
through carelessness, but by intention—there is no particular point in saving it, unless, again, for some immediate purpose ;  never for any indefinite future purpose.
Money will never be a matter of great importance to
them, nothing more than a convenient medium of exchange.

Sex is not a disturbing matter for them.   They have
probably both had sexual experience.   If so, it has been
with their own kind, experimental or in a love episode.
There has been nothing degrading about it and they may
carry into their marriage memories that they will always
cherish.   Sex has never been a hidden secret to them, it
did not burst upon them unawares in adolescence.   It has
been a natural part of life, like all other parts of life,
with no special importance attached to it through mystery.
It is not a " dirty " subject and they have no notion
of its being " sacred ", or of the " sacredness " of their
bodies or of " God's intentions " in regard to them.   For
them a sexual relation in addition to being a physical
relief of tensions that have become uncomfortable is the
consummation of a love experience that they find vitalizing and stimulating and with this as justification enough
they are ready to enter into it fully and without self-
consciousness.

Pregnancy is no hindrance in their relationship.   They
are well informed  in regard to birth-control measures

and if for any reason (it will not be financial) they do not for the present wish a child, these measures will be used. If even so the wife becomes pregnant there is no dismay, for an abortion may be obtained at the local hospital, or special clinic, under the best and safest conditions.

If the child is desired the mother will continue with her work, if she remains well, until within four to six weeks of her confinement, after which she will remain at home but without any loss of pay. She will be delivered in a hospital and when sufficiently recovered will return with the child to her home to remain another four to six weeks, again without loss of pay. From the beginning of the pregnancy to her confinement she will have been under the supervision of the pre-natal clinic, and from her delivery to her return to work, longer if necessary, under the supervision of the maternity clinic. The child will remain under the supervision of the maternity and child clinic until it is four years of age. When the mother returns from the hospital she brings with her *a wanted child*.

PRE-SCHOOL LIFE : AMERICAN

The mother knows more about algebra, Latin, or if she has been to a university, Elizabethan literature and the French dramatists (or once did ; she no longer attends to them) than the physical and psychological care of her child, about which she knows nothing whatsoever. In preparation for her job as typist or secretary she spent at least several months of intensive application in learning ; in preparation for motherhood she may have " read a book " on the simpler physical needs of the child. Because of her lack of knowledge there will be a good deal of unnecessary anxiety in regard to the child. She will soon swing between moods of overdevotion to the child and irritation at its incessant demands and its confinement of her. Nursing will probably not be a pleasure for her and she will make many mistakes in the process that will have lasting effects on the character and personality of the child. She will put an end to the process as soon as possible and probably much sooner than should be for the best interests, physical and psychological, of the child. Expenses will mount with Grade A milk and an occasional visit from the doctor. Toilet habits will be established with " shame ", " dirty ", " nasty ", " ugh ", with important results in the character and personality of the child—at twenty-five, and the time of its marriage ; at thirty-five when now a promising young professor, chief of clinic, rising barrister or priest ; at forty-five, fifty-five when now full professor, leading " specialist ", judge, archbishop, it will still be trying to form some compromise between interests never outgrown and the " ugh " of its mother—and what queer forms it will take in professor, judge, archbishop, and how they will veer in the performance of their public duties from these interests to " ugh ".

If the mother finds her child rubbing its penis, or showing any curiosity about this organ, she will probably be in a panic, and to punish it there will be another round of " naughty ", " bad ", " shame ", for which later the professor, judge, archbishop will pay.

The child will be taught to pray ; not that the mother or father have any interest in prayer, but the mother will feel vaguely that perhaps the child ought anyway to " say its prayers " every night. As time goes on there will be questions from the child about this mysterious

person God, and the Father, and the Holy Ghost, and the
Son, and Jesus Christ, and the Virgin Mary and innumer-
able " miracle-working " individuals who have become
saints, the answers to which the mother will have to make
up out of whole cloth, for it is still completely confusing
to her ; but out of her vague answers the child will build
something for himself in fantasy.  And this will live to
plague him.  A bit later even worse plagues will be prepared for him when it comes to explanations of sex.

During this period the father will be a puzzle to the
child.  The mother is more or less just another part of
himself, a curiously satisfying and a strangely unsatisfying self, but altogether more satisfactory than the father
who is no part of himself, at most only an unpleasant
part of the part-self mother.  This will be so regardless
of the affectionate attitude of the father.

Although for the past year the greatest care has been
used, even to the point of unsatisfying sexual relations,
that the wife should not again become pregnant—another
child simply cannot be afforded at this time—the wife
does become pregnant.  In this year or two years the
child has learned how to get what it wants and rules
with considerable despotism.  It has been the one object
of interest in an adult household consisting not only of
parents but grandparents, aunts and uncles and family
friends.  From these it has learned to talk and walk, to
show off its antics ; also how to obtain unearned and un-
deserved rewards through coercion.  With the advent of
the new brother or sister the world will sadly change and
not without producing effects in the form of resentment
and jealousy.  Before he is off to school there will be more
children ; the rise in the father's salary will not be com-
mensurate with the rise in expense ; greater anxiety,

querulousness, continued sexual frustration, irritation with occasional temper explosions, tears will come into the household and create an atmosphere that will be communicated. At four or five, if the family can afford it, there will be kindergarten; at six or seven, school.

The mother will not have had any Latin to forget and she will probably not be much better informed about her child than the American mother. Although not necessarily so. The child is not just something that happened but is a wanted, planned-for child, and a child in Russia is very important; it is a welcome unit in a social structure and has a public, not alone a personal-parental, importance. But whether she knows more or less than the American mother, does not so greatly matter. When she returns to her work she will bring the child with her, if there is a nursery there, or, if not, she will leave it on her way to work at a neighbouring nursery. The nursery will be in charge of trained people who do know more than the American mother. They will not be " starched professionals " with a minimum of interest in the children under their care, who must work to maintain themselves and have chosen this means as the least disagreeable of those open to them, but women who have little interest in, or need to have interest in, the monetary return for their work, and who, because of their interest in children, have chosen this form of social contribution. Children are to them not just something towards which one performs a professional duty but individuals of very great social potential. At regular intervals during the day, without loss of pay, the mother will come to the nursery, put on a sterilized gown and have a quiet half-hour nursing her baby.

At the end of the day she will return home with it. And she will return not to another day's work in the home, for there the work has been done for her. After a busy but not exhausting day at work, without a thousand and one things to do before bedtime, she is free to relax with her child and to give him of her best before his bedtime. Under these conditions the babe is a joy from which she can receive much and to which she can give generously and unreservedly.

The child will continue its life in the nursery and eventually in the kindergarten. It will never be an " only " child. It will never be the centre of an adult world. From its earliest days it will be a part of its own age group. From the time it begins to crawl it will be crawling with others, learning from others and with others. There will never be a time when others will burst in upon its world as strangers or when it will be propelled into their world as a stranger. It will never know strangers, and potential enemies, in that sense—for it will always have been with others and from the simplest beginnings and relationships will have learned how to get on with others of its own age. It will not need to develop, because of fear, ugly defensive habits of aggression or equally bad habits of withdrawal, or of placating others with excessive generousness, kindliness and sweetness (which, although it seems so acceptable, is not, of course, sound because it is not a true expression but a personality trait built out of weakness, rather than out of strength).

The child will not be left insecure through lack of affection. This it will receive from the mother substitutes at the nursery, but it will be an intelligent affection that cannot be coerced ; most generously, however, it will receive the love of its parents and its parents will be the centre of its world although it will never be as completely dependent upon them as children who have no other form of security.

It will not be taught to pray. It will be led to discover the world about it and to busy itself in that world. Nothing will be " dirty ", " nasty ", " wicked ", " shameful ", " mamma cry "—*except* that gradually it will become somehow aware that the one thing that does not seem to be acceptable is browbeating or bullying ; a little later will come another distinction, that it isn't aggressiveness in itself that is disapproved but an aggression in one's own interest at the cost of another's ; still later it will come to learn the word " exploitation " and this will be the beginning of the formulation of a moral code.

His moral code will always remain simple and thoroughly understandable to him. It will be built up from his own experience within the group and will in no way be confused with the wishes of a vague, mysterious something called a God, who is said to be all Love, whatever that may be, and yet is somehow fearful and awesome ; who, in spite of such love and interest, is approachable (for most people) only through a hierarchy of earthly representatives, most of whom on any other ground one would not respect at all, and heavenly representatives, quite inexplicable ; and Whose wishes seem often so contrary to the wishes He is supposed to have put in him, the explanation of which is so complicated, even amusing, if it were not all so solemn ; and to all of which no one will really seem to attach much importance, only grow solemn when the subjects are mentioned and lower their voices a bit . . . all of which will be very confusing at a time when these things are important to him and he has not yet learned to dismiss them and find more intelligent explanations or to accept them with indifference as beyond his comprehension and, going through the forms, let it go at that.

There will be none of this to confuse the Russian child as he begins to construct his relationship to himself, to others and to the universe as a whole. Nothing mysterious and complicated to learn ; nothing to unlearn. From experience he will learn that intelligent and honest people are simple, direct and approachable ; that façades of pompousness, solemnity and dignity are to hide weakness or emptiness ; that the more important the thing, the simpler is its fundamental explanation : that complicated explanations are but wordy dust to hide ignorance. He will early give his confidence, therefore, to those who can explain to him the things he wants to know and with this start will continue to find explanations, his relationship to others remaining simple and direct because nothing artificial requires that it be otherwise.

### SCHOOL : AMERICAN

Our average American boy will go to the public school. It will be well equipped and the teachers will be well trained in the teaching of their particular subject. They will, indeed, know much more about their " subject " than about the children under their direction. They will have had a course in " psychology " in their normal school training but this will be quite remote from the children before them, or even " child psychology " which will not be very real, or " educational psychology " which will have to do more with how to get the stuff in than with the child as a whole who is to take the dose. But regardless

of how much they may know about children and of their
interest in them, they will have little opportunity to
utilize this knowledge, for their classes will be seriously
overcrowded ; there will be direct and heavy pressure
from above for certain tangible results by the calendar
and, contend as they may against all these difficulties,
their work will become more and more routine and they
more and more distraught and under tension with the
continued over-work and frustration of their ideals.

Our boy, or girl, may enter school as a new experience
with enthusiasm, or, if it is his first experience with a
group, with dread.   For most it will be the first experience
with the group and the group lessons will be much more
difficult than class-room lessons.   The child will learn
to bluff, to get its own way by force or subterfuge, or to
protect itself by retreat or capitulation, or by building
castles of " idealism " in which it can stow itself away,
superior to its more forceful contemporaries.   It will have
no particular purpose in going to school.   There will be
nothing there that it will be particularly excited about
learning.   In so far as it learns at all it will learn because
it must.   School is a place where all children must go
between certain ages and once there one doesn't want
to appear any dumber than necessary and so a certain
amount of work one must do.   There will be rivalry, of
a purely personal kind, to be better than someone else,
just to be better.   Comparisons will constantly be made.
A really dull child will soon be quite unhappy.   A bright
child is likely to become quite unbearable.   The spirit
that soon will dominate will be that of passing in a
subject, moving into a higher form, getting on ; not
because of any content but because of the calendar and
pride.   Parents will have little interest in the curriculum.

They will be very much interested in whether the child passes its examinations in proper order and time and possibly where it stands in relation to others. Problems will arise between pupil and teacher, between pupil and pupil, between child and parent and these will be settled by scolding, punishment, appeal to vague moral principles which seem always to work in the other fellow's interest, to pride, to duty (how he has come upon this duty not being very clear), to responsibility (when and where he assumed these responsibilities being also not very clear) and finally again to threat and more punishment. Little or no effort will be made to understand what is confusing the child and causing it to react defensively as it does. It will be a " bad " child if it does not do what is expected of it and a " good " child if it does. In neither case will the conduct be an expression of the real child, but all, including the child, will assume it to be, and with this false start the child enters upon its conquering of the world.

There will be heroes. Washington and Lincoln will be the big heroes, in fact men so good and so wise as to be almost beyond emulation. There will be Garfield and the rise from the canal-boat to the presidency. There will be a great deal about boys who from humble beginnings have risen " to the top "—that is what America means, unequalled opportunity for everyone who is honest and works hard to " get to the top ". There will be many examples of this. His greatest personal heroes, however, will probably be athletes or movie stars—someone who has worked himself out from the mass and stands brilliantly revealed for all the world to see, perhaps even a racketeer. The most ridiculous persons, or somehow the most wicked or fearsome persons, will be

" radicals " who are always saying such awful and untrue things about the most sacred and important things.

There will be confusion about friends from school. The nice little Italian boy turns out to be something called a " Dago " which means something that isn't nice. The little Jewish boy is, of course, just as good as anyone else and so is the little negro boy, but mother would prefer that they were not brought home. The little boy across the street whose father is a doctor is a very nice little boy, the mother thinks, although her son knows him as a dirty-minded little bully. But somehow he is held preferable.

Honesty, honour and truth-telling are emphasized in school and in the Sunday school and also by the parents. But before very long it is perfectly evident from what has been seen and heard at home that in some curious way distinctions are to be made. To cheat in school is something awful, but from father's conversation of how he put something over, even sometimes from mother's conversation, cheating isn't always wrong ; although when it isn't wrong, it isn't called cheating, although it seems so much like it.

There will be some " music " and some " art " taught in the school but it will not be considered important. These will be " cultural " subjects. The teachers will be so occupied getting in the required amount of grammar, arithmetic and composition that they will have little time to take note of any particularly talented child. And there could be little done about it if they did, as the school offers no real opportunity for such a child. A teacher is likely to be annoyed by a talented child who is half-heartedly, or with no heart at all, applying itself to

the school routine. Eventually, however, the majority
will have managed to gather a satisfactory knowledge of
the primary subjects and they will pass on into the high
school.

SCHOOL : UNION OF SOVIET SOCIALIST REPUBLICS

To the Russian child school will not be an institution
for children but an adult institution to which it can now
be admitted.  It can probably not recall a time when
someone about was not studying.  It has grown up in
the presence of study—father studies, mother studies,
perhaps even grandfather and grandmother study, all
the neighbours study, everybody studies, there seems to
be no end to it, one can always study, studying isn't just
something one does during a certain period and then,
" finished ", " graduated ", be through with it for ever.
There is, further, something in the school he wants to get.
From the life in the nursery, the kindergarten, the home,
he has picked up what is probably at the moment not
much more than a feeling that it is important to know
things.  He is already aware that he is a part of whatever
is.  Already he and his group have done things and there
are other things to do.  But one must know how.  As
all the others who do things go to school, school must be
the place where one can learn.

There will be few problems to solve between him and
his fellow pupils, either boy or girl.  They have been
accustomed to each other since they were two months old.
Personal rivalry plays little part.  The one most respected
is the one most identified with the group, who can think
best and direct best.  His leadership arouses no animosity
or jealousy on the part of others, as they elected him and
he merely carries out their plans.  His position is no more

important than theirs; there is merely a difference in function. Distinctions in grades of importance through position are strange to him. It is the group as a whole and the work as a whole that is important and everyone in the group is as important as anyone else in the group, although duties and functions may be different. As long as he does his best in the group, even though he may not be as bright as some of the others, he can have perfect self-respect, for others will give him their respect, and there need be no feeling of difference that he must make up in some way.

The school will not be as well equipped nor the teachers, theoretically at least, as well trained as in America, and the classes for the moment will be mostly too large. But there will be no denial that this is so and it will be remedied as rapidly as possible. There will be few problems between the teacher and the pupil, the teacher and the parent, or the pupil and the parent. And for a very simple reason—they all have the same purpose. The school is but a part of a larger whole of which they are all a part, and is not an end in itself but a means to an end. And this end is nothing vague such as " culture ", knowledge for its own sake, steps in personal " progress ", " learning how to live ", " preparation for life ", and the like. It is definitely so to organize social life that a satisfying life, one worth living, will be possible for all, this to be accomplished through co-operative effort and the doing away with all forms of exploitation. There will be no confusion between anything taught at school and what is daily acted out in the home or the community. As life extends and social contacts become more intricate, moral principles will extend also to meet new situations, but they will remain simple and understandable, being but the extension of the fundamental principle that there shall be no exploitation.

There will be heroes. Lenin and Karl Marx will be the great heroes. But with this interesting and significant difference. The heroes we create for our children are personalities so presented as to form examples—hence the interest in the personal lives of these individuals (to be patched up where necessary), their rugged honesty, their struggles and suffering in standing for the right, their final overcoming of all difficulties and their passage to the God who has directed them and upon Whom they have leaned at all times. The object is to make children " good ". In Russia the object is to make them think. It is Lenin's and Karl Marx's ideas that are important, not their personal lives. Perhaps they did suffer and go through many privations. One would expect that they did ; thousands have done that in the name of the Revolution in Russia for a hundred or more years ; there is nothing special in that. The personal lives of individuals belong to them, whether neighbour or hero, and are unimportant except to themselves, but what they may have discovered or invented or thought that helps to a better understanding of the world, makes simpler the work of the world or more intelligent the organization of the social world—that is important and one cannot know enough.

Sex will begin to play its part in the grade school. But it is more likely to be a constructive form of sexual growth, rather than the dirty-minded snickering sort due to frustrated curiosity trying to find out about something that is known to be not nice, even wicked. The Russian child has known about sex since nursery days. There has never been anything special about it. Boys and girls have grown up together. They have known of their physical difference, but of no other differences except as there are differences between all individuals. The differences are not upon a sexual basis but upon the basis of ability and talent and interest. What is expected of each is their best, and boy or girl is therefore free to do what he or she can best do. The best of everything is needed whether it be building a stone wall, the writing of a song, the repairing of an engine, the cooking of a meal or the embroidering of a shirt. All these things are necessary in the total life of the group. If what one does is needed and is good then that is as important, honourable and praiseworthy as what someone else does well that is needed. In the last analysis there are no relative importances. At any given moment one thing may be more important than another, the fixing of a roof in a storm, or, in the present moment in Russia generally, the building of factories and the construction of tractors, reapers, trucks and automobiles, but it is quite understood that this is a temporary matter and is of greater importance only for the moment because of circumstances and is not really more important than other things.

It is too early to say what the effect of this attitude will be, but there is reason to expect very great effects in the psychology of certain children that should make not only for greater personal happiness, but for social peace and the enrichment of life in general. The boy who is not sufficiently strong to build stone walls, but through whose head go continually chains of words in rhythm, or scraps of melody, or whose muscles sway naturally into dance, may proceed along his course without any defence of his personality. He will, indeed, be helped and urged on, thoroughly appreciated by his comrades.

And the girl whose strength is such that needlework would leave her distracted by unused energy may build stone walls or run a tractor, again without any defence of her personality. Particularly will it be important in the amelioration of the castration trauma. Every Russian girl, as every American girl, will, upon the discovery of the male penis, receive a trauma. She will react to this trauma with jealousy, envy, hate, guilt, fear and anxiety. And what then? Daily salt will be rubbed into the wound of the American girl. She will be reminded on every hand that she is different and not only different, but inferior. Words to the contrary will help little or not at all—the facts are too obvious. To defend herself she will erect various psychological defences until, in the end, her psychological life, and thereby her social life, will become so complicated, there will be so many drives and counter-drives within her, none of which she can accurately evaluate, that only a life of tumult and frustration is possible for her. The little Russian girl will receive also her trauma, but from that day on there will be little or no salt to the wound. Not words but the facts about her will indicate that while there is a difference, as between many things, there is no inferiority and that she is free to express herself simply and directly. No defence is needed.

Throughout these school days special talents will be searched for—talents, all talents, are needed. The teachers are not working to get the students into the high school, they are helping to build a civilization, and not indirectly, oratorically by way of commencement addresses, but directly. And they take their job seriously. Every child is a unit in that structure, a unit of unknown potential. No job is more important than the discovery

and utilization of that potential. It is not that they in
their professional pride (defence) say so, *everyone* says
so. Every effort will be made therefore, from observation, special examination, to personal conference, to
discover what these special talents are—and once found,
music, drawing, modelling, technical, the way is opened
up for the progress of the child. The distance a child
may go along the line of its special talent is determined
alone by the amount of that talent. And if in the end
—and this is to be remembered—that talent is found to
have a limit and the individual never writes the opera
he had hoped, or sings in the Moscow opera, or becomes
the chief surgeon in a great clinic, he does not thereby
become a disillusioned, disappointed, sour second-rater.
It was never his *primary* intention to become the greatest
tenor, the greatest painter, the greatest surgeon of Russia.
This as it may be. His ambition has been to help build
a Communistic state. And in this he has succeeded.
There has been no failure. His singing, his writing, his
work as a surgeon has been his way, through a special
talent, of making his contribution. Those who have
exceeded him have done no more than he, for they, like
him, have only done their best. Because his talent was
less than theirs he is not blameworthy.

The grade school for the Russian child has been truly
an experience in living, and living not in an artificial
world, as so often is the case in our progressive schools,
but living in a real world, the world of his parents and
of his community. He has continued to learn how to
get on with others, how to work with the group, how to
follow, how perhaps to lead ; he has begun to develop
a moral code and a philosophy of life in harmony with
his environment, he has perhaps begun to get some inkling

of his special interests and talents and along what line he can probably best make his contribution ; he has learned a great deal about the actual world and wants to know more ; he has learned a great deal about what is going on in the world—not only in Russia but throughout the world, a surprising amount—and of the great men and women of the world, the scientists who have discovered things and made the world more understandable and life upon it easier, the great artists and musicians who have helped to express life ; and with this his grammar, composition and arithmetic, only these have never been just grammar, composition and arithmetic but ways of doing things.

### HIGH SCHOOL : AMERICAN

During the high-school period the American boy or girl will be supposed to give his or her interested attention to Latin, German, French, mathematics, English literature, one or more historical periods, and the like, but this will not be quite possible because of what has preceded. Their intellectual preparation has been adequate and their discipline—things are done because they are done, not for any particular reason—is fairly good, but, unknown to most teachers and parents, a reckoning-time has now come, and at a very unfavourable period because there are things now that they ought to be doing, with concentrated attention and undistracted ; but these things —pursuit of studies necessary in their intellectual advancement—must now have second place while the youth struggles with all the emotional contradictions, uncertainties and rationalizations that his home, school, church and communal life have woven into his being, in order to bring some sort of harmony into his personality. This will be a mighty struggle in the dark that will often leave little energy for the subjects he is supposed to be studying.

There will be little reason to apply what energy he has to what is laid before him, unless as a defence he has become cowardly and does what he is told without asking for reasons. He will never know why he is study-ing Latin—except perhaps that it is required if he is to pass into a university, nor why he is studying algebra or geometry, except for the same reason. Nor will he know why it is required by the university except that it always has been. He will study French or German without knowing why, except that another language is required, for no one, not even his medical or Ph.D. friends, seem ever to show any interest in a language once they have " studied " it. The study of his French or German or Spanish (for commercial reasons ! !) will be apparently on the unspoken assumption that he is to become a philologist and will, therefore, be made as difficult and uninteresting and impracticable as possible. After his year's struggle with grammar there will be some senti-mental stories to read or some legends which, with his still limited experience of history will be boring ; both will be old and filled with obsolete words which he will faithfully look up and try to remember—just as the German youth searches out the meanings of the obsolete words and grammatical forms of Washington Irving. So do we come to appreciate German and American culture. With the linguistic understanding of a native seven- or eight-year-old child we are expected to appreciate the beauties or even to discover the profundities of Dickens, Shakespeare, Goethe and Schiller. After a try at it the youth will understand better why his father and mother have never done anything more with the German or

French they once studied ; but he will still insist later that his own son go through the same performance and call him lazy and indifferent when he balks at it.

There will be history, one or more periods—Ancient History, Greek History, Roman History, History of the Middle Ages, Modern European History, English History, American History, all carefully departmentalized, so carefully, indeed, that for a youth studying English or American history other countries will not exist except as they are incidentally involved now and then politically.  The history in each instance will be the history of politics. There will be a bow now and then to other matters but the things to be remembered will be political.  And the subjects will be taught as though the aim of the student was to become an historian.

There will be science, mostly rather feebly taught, or, if there are well-organized departments of Physics, Chemistry, Biology, each very much with a capital letter, each will be as much a stranger to the other as the Equator and the North Pole.  Each will be " pure ", detached, impersonal, as unliving as Latin.

And there will be other subjects, all things in themselves, all taught as though the youth were to become a specialist in that subject, unliving, " courses " one has to take or to elect for a credit.  For those not desiring or unable to go to universities, no matter how capable they may be or how much they may desire it, there will be trade and " white-collar " courses that will put their feet on the first rung of the ladder that will make it possible for them to become big business men—if they are honest and industrious.  Here and there, not infrequently, in fact, but accidentally, unplanned, unappreciated mostly, for such teachers are likely to interfere with well-running machinery, there will be a teacher who, out of the richness of his or her personality, fundamental grasp of subject and, above all, knowledge and appreciation of and respect for youth, will extend an horizon, open up a vista, make the subject and related subjects live, make from apparently chaotic and unrelated things a synthesis that will be the start of intellectual growth for some youth. Many, however, perhaps most, will have been so dulled by the process through which they have been going for the past ten or twelve years that they will be unable to respond or to respond but feebly.

But, for a rare exception, or unless our youth has failed in making adequate contact with the life about him and as compensation has thrown himself into being a " good " student and probably also a " good " boy as a means of showing his disapproval of the things in which he finds himself unable to take part, our youth will not be greatly concerned about his " subjects ". His preoccupation will be with " getting himself over ", with being recognized, with being somebody, often with being elected to something as evidence of success and popularity. There will be many drives and forces, counter-drives and counter-forces in his make-up. He is now an " adolescent problem ", often recognized as such by his bizarre conduct, often not recognized as such because he is " popular " and getting on, or is gracious and amenable.

With his " credits " stowed away, but with little intellectual interest, his ability to think still undeveloped, emotionally confused, unwilling longer to remain so closely dependent upon the home but fearful of entering into a larger world (and with emotionally dependent parents, full of anxiety and fear—of what ?—that he will make a misstep and not be " good " and thereby injure his chances of getting on—making the problem as difficult as possible), devious and guilty in his sexual interests, perhaps with " ideals ", but with ideals developed mostly in defence of his weaknesses rather than as an expression of his strengths, or, still more likely, with no interests, no purpose, no goal, no aim except a personal ambition to get somewhere and to be someone, he enters college for four more years of " subjects ".   And in the end we expect him to be a " good " man, a good husband, a good father, a good citizen who will help to lead the world toward the good life.

Q. E. D.

### HIGH SCHOOL : UNION OF SOVIET SOCIALIST REPUBLICS

The Russian youth will come to the high school prepared to work.   The grade school has led him into a world of things, of people, of activity.   It has already shown him a great deal about that world and particularly has it shown him how he may approach that world more closely.   Everything he has done has been a step leading into that world, or the creation of tools with which to discover that world, and *this relationship* has been clear to him.   Lessons have not just been " lessons " and subjects " subjects " with no particular relationship to anything else.   He has learned surprisingly well how to think, how to plan for himself, how to seek help either from the group or from his instructor ;  he has begun to form some notion of what interests him, of what his special talents may be and of what, in view of his talents, he would like to do as his contribution to the work of the group.   If he has no outstanding talents, indeed if he is a bit dull, he still will have found, or will be on the way to finding what he does best.   His lack of ability in mathematics may make it impracticable to think of becoming an engineer ; but one can be just as useful as a mechanic and one can be a good mechanic.[1]

His personality will be comparatively uncomplicated. It has developed so gradually and naturally that it comes as near being a true representation of himself as it is now probably possible to be. Little has gone into it to create artificial conflict within himself and little to magnify such natural conflicts as must exist. He will have little emotionally to unlearn, few habits to change, certainly no complete re-orientation to make. In his relationship to himself, his contemporaries, his family, the community as a whole, he is already well oriented and a continued growth upon the lines already established is all that is

[1] It is interesting to note that this decision in regard to lack of ability in mathematics is made by the boy and not by his instructors. The instructors will, of course, have pointed this out to him—not as an inferiority but as a difference—and will have suggested that he will probably find the mathematics required for engineering too difficult for him. If the boy himself is not convinced of this, however, he will be permitted to proceed until he proves the matter to his own satisfaction. He will not nurse this as a personal disappointment, for, during this period, his " social " training will be continued, very specially, perhaps, because the special need will be recognized and the instructors value this boy as a social unit of still unknown potentiality and are desirous that he find the place where he can contribute best. This training will consist in making it clearer to him—and in this they are not " kidding him " as one would be doing here but are really pointing out a reality to him—that his difference is not an inferiority, that every ability is needed, that the group can only make progress through the application of all talent and that all that is required is one's best at any point in the combined activity. The boy will not have great difficulty in accepting this for it will be not just the encouraging words of an innocent unworldly-wise teacher but an expression of what he sees about him in his daily life. *That* plus the tactful guidance at school send him on at his best.

required.   Such new problems as there will be will have
to do with his physical growth and increasing sex consciousness.   But this is simplified for him in that it is
only a *sex consciousness* with which he has to deal, not a
*self consciousness*.   Consciousness of sex is an uncomplicated reality problem which he can not only accept
but welcome, and the basis for his handling of it has been
in the process of being built since he was a child—in
the method he has been taught of handling any reality
problem (learn about it, not fear and dodge it, avoid and
deny it), in his frankness, directness and openness in
dealing with others, in his knowledge of and relationship
to girls which is not new, his knowledge of sex, which is
not new and which has never been smutty, and in his
one all-embracing moral principle, no exploitation ; this,
together with his general social viewpoint and his already
stimulated interest in knowledge and learning and the
application of this knowledge to social group activity,
makes adolescence a not particularly difficult period.
There will be things to distract him, but these will be
reality situations which in themselves are a part of learning
so long as they remain reality situations, and not conflicts
within himself from which he can learn nothing but
become only the more confused.   In so far as is possible,
without turning a reality problem into a problem of
personal conflict, the school and the community will help
in this adolescent sex situation.

Some Americans at the time of my last visit were
surprised to find bathers in the rivers at Leningrad and
Moscow wearing trunks.   They were inclined to be
indignant.   They had expected the Russians to be
" normal " and " natural " and free of all such Puritanical
" moral bunk ".   There had always been nude bathing

in Russia. Why now trunks? The reply was that the problem was not a " moral " one but a purely practical one. Earlier the Russian view had been the same as that expressed by the Americans, and there had been complete freedom ; there was now no " moral " feeling and no law against nude bathing ; plenty of nude bathers would be found, and without any interference the Americans could now throw off their clothing and jump into the river if they wanted to do so ; that the Russians were not, however, like the Americans, " idealists ", in the sense that an idea once held as an ideal must always be held in spite of all evidence that it did not work, in fact, perhaps that it complicated the problem it was intended to solve ; the Russians were " realists", in the sense that they wanted things to work and that an idea raised to an ideal had no value, in fact was harmful if it did not produce the thing desired. The idea behind nude bathing had been health, pleasure and the minimizing of self-consciousness in the matter of sex, in the hope that this would help in the solving of so-called " sex " problems, that so far as adults or children were concerned this might be accomplished ; it had been found, however, that it increased the problem of the adolescent ; again, not that there was any " moral " feeling about this, not that there was any desire that the adolescent should not be sexually stimulated—they expected him to be ; how indeed could he develop naturally otherwise? Adolescence, however, was an important time for learning and they wished the adolescent to be as emotionally and physically free for learning as, in the nature of the circumstances, he could be ; that, under the circumstances, he could not be completely free they understood and accepted and were willing to let natural sexual stimulation take its course as a part of the learning process ; that all they wished to avoid was overstimulation that would so preoccupy the attention of the adolescent as to handicap him at a critical learning period ; that it had been found that mixed naked bathing among adolescents was overstimulating and that therefore there was a growing consensus of opinion, although no law, against naked bathing in the cities and that in the Pioneer camps (boy and girl adolescents) the wearing of trunks was required ; that this was the *idea* of the moment, that it represented nothing fixed into an " ideal " ; if it helped towards accomplishing the purpose in mind, which was a practical and not a " moral " purpose, it would continue to be held, whereas if it were found not to work it would be discarded and an effort made to find some other way.

It is interesting to note that some of the Americans were not convinced by what seemed to be a quite reasonable argument. So accustomed were they, once having decided that something was " right " (the primary decision as to what was " right " being determined, of course, wholly unobjectively and wholly on the grounds of a personal conflict), to stick to it as an " ideal " through thick and thin (for, of course, representing a personal conflict it must be stuck to until the conflict is resolved and a conflict cannot be resolved by any argument or presentation of evidence) and to continue to insist that the Russians were betraying their cause and would eventually become as nasty minded as vice crusaders. The Americans became quite emotionally overheated (showing the personal nature of the problem) ; the Russians remained quite calm in the face of a really ugly attack (further evidence that with them it was not a personal problem).

It is interesting and probably not unprofitable to carry speculation a little further.

Had it come to an issue the Americans would probably have taken off their clothes and gone into the river to *demonstrate their freedom from any false modesty*, the very need of the demonstration, however, proving their real lack of freedom and the extent to which they must go to deny their conflict. The Russians, quite free of such sexual conflict, potent in sexual relations, and able without embarrassment on any necessary or suitable occasion to appear unclothed, would probably have remained clothed on the bank and watched calmly the American demonstration, even accepted smilingly the accusations that they did not " dare " to take off their clothes and that their unwillingness to do so " proved " that their sexual freedom was a fake. Just so upside-down is the world.

But it will not be into such an upside-down world that the Russian youth will go as he enters high school. It will be a world not regulated by theories and " ideals " long out-worn, but a world regulated by the realities of the situation. There will be no solemn, long-faced, but very funny talk about " culture " or the " cultural value " of certain subjects. In the first place, there will not be much interest in what we call " culture " (all too often the rather refined and precious use as an end of what is really a means to an end). It will be held that those who build a " culture " upon the exploitation of others cannot themselves be very cultured. That this boy and his contemporaries, it will be held in the second place, may build a culture and themselves become cultured, no false cross-cuts will be taken but instruments will be put into their hands—and as instruments. There will be no pretence that " culture " can be induced by four years of high school and four years at a university, and instead of wasting these years in such effort they will be utilized in laying the groundwork for a culture that can develop throughout the boy's entire life.

He will study Latin—if Latin can be of any use to him in his plans ; otherwise, not.  He will have opportunity to study English, German and French.  If he elects to study any one or more of these languages, however, it will be assumed that he does so because he wishes to use them (not that he desires to become a philologist) and they will be taught in as practicable a way as possible, utilizing the vocabulary and the grammatical constructions which those who speak these languages use daily and omitting those things that the average Englishman, German or Frenchman finds it unnecessary to know.  A foundation will be laid, however, upon which he can build as extensive a knowledge of the language as he may later desire or have need for.

He will study such mathematics as will be of use to him.  If he is not going to a university it will probably not be much ; the time will be given to other subjects that will be useful to him.  If he is going to a university it will depend upon what he plans to do there.  Boys and girls do not just go to universities in Russia.  Universities are open to all, but if one chooses to go it is because there is something there one desires to get.  To go to a university in order to " kill time ", to " have a good time ", to get " culture ", to have evidence of being a " gentleman ", of making friends who will " be helpful later ", of becoming an athletic " hero " would be unthinkable in Russia.  To do so a youth would have to violate all that he had learned since he was two months

old, and at the university he would not find what he
was looking for.

One of the most interesting subjects, however, will
probably be history.  He has already had a good deal of
history and what he studies in the high school will be a
continuation.  The history he has been having, and of
which he will now have more detail, will be the history
of the physical world, the development of life upon the
world, the struggle men have had to understand themselves and their world, the steps in this process, the men
and women who have contributed to knowledge of the
world, the nature and history of these contributions and
to what they have led, the history of world organization,
of the relationship of individual to individual and of
peoples to peoples, the rise of industrialism with the new
knowledge, of the use of power and wealth thus created,
nationalism and internationalism, the nature and function of religion and " culture " and " philosophy " and
" patriotism " in this total process.  There will be little
political history.  The life of men from the earliest beginnings to the present will be divided into large periods
representing certain steps in people (not national) relationships and quite different from our classical divisions
along cultural and political lines.  Most of what American
boys find in their histories and learn for examination will
be material for footnotes only, or as passing illustration
for the text.  That a group of American exploiters (good
men in the light of their philosophy, and their exploitation mostly legal) should desire to be free from the
exploitation of George III, in order that they might have
greater freedom for their own exploitation, will not be
considered a very important point in the history of men
—just a further example of a well-known story.  That

Dalton first determined the atomic weights of elements, that Volta developed the electric pile, the work of Darwin, of Pasteur, of Einstein will be considered of the very greatest importance, not as physics or chemistry or bacteriology or whatnot but as history. That a man once said he was the " Son of God " and died on a cross to " save " men will be considered of no importance at all, and will be reserved for special study in the history and function of religions. Edison and the workers in the field of electro-dynamics, however, will far eclipse Napoleon whose entire career can be confined to a footnote as again merely one of thousands of illustrations of a monotonous story. In the end the Russian boy will not know as many facts as the American boy at the time of his examination (neither will the American boy six months later), but such facts as he knows will have a significance for him, which cannot be said for the American boy. And he may have as many facts, although they will be very different facts, and he will not so readily forget them because they do have real significance for him.

There will be music, various forms of art work, possibly dancing. These will not be given as minor subjects for their " cultural " value, but as major subjects because of their usefulness. A student will not be forced beyond his talents in these subjects—although if he has special talent there will be no limit to its development. They will be presented to him not as " art ", but as different forms of expression which he may use himself in expressing his ideas, if the form is suitable for him, or which at least he can understand as others express their ideas to him in these forms ; he will be shown that they are more adequate for the expression of some ideas than ordinary forms of speech or writing and that, indeed, some, with no talent for speech or writing, would find it impossible to communicate their ideas except for these forms.

Apart from his " subjects " he will be very busy. From nursery days he has done " social work ". Year by year this has become more important in its form, and with greater community value, until now, in the high school, it may have very wide ramifications into the life of the community. " Social work " consists of activities undertaken by the individual or group, without recompense, that are of value to the community as a whole. What this will be in any given instance will depend upon the immediate needs of the community. It may be teaching illiterate adults, directing the work of younger communist groups, inspecting certain community services, the preparation or care of a public playground, the planting and care of shrubs and flowers in public parks and streets. He is on hand and ready for all sorts of calls ranging from manual labour to various kinds of intellectual work. There will be activities within his school group, activities with the larger group to which he belongs outside the school, all of these socially oriented. In these various activities there will be no attempt to put himself forward as a leader. He has no need to " get himself across " as a leader. He is " across ". His place is secure. Leadership is a serious and burdensome responsibility. He will not refuse it, neither fear nor false modesty (he would scarcely know what " modesty " was in that sense) will cause him to dodge responsibility. He will accept it if the group is agreed upon him, but as a responsibility for carrying out the ideas of the group. He had been chosen because the group believes he can get done what the group wants done. If it is discovered that he lacks this special ability another will replace him. Neither the group, nor he, is bothering itself about honours or this or that. What it wants is to get something done and it is looking for a leader able to bring this about.

At the end of his school period, if the boy is not to go to a university, he will take the place he has prepared himself for—there will be no period of looking for a job. He has already been on his job for some time, for the school has its connections with the various community activities and a part of his instruction has been in connection with these. His name is now merely transferred from the school roll to the work- and payroll.

If he plans to enter a university to prepare himself as engineer, physician, teacher, scientist, he will first, after passing his examinations, devote two years to work. This will mean mostly work in a factory or upon a communal farm. The work may have some relationship to his future work or it may not. At least, it will not be the temporary work of the dilettante—it will have nothing of the rich man's son " learning the business " about it. It will be work and as others work. There will be no distinction between him and any other worker. To most, Communism, as exemplified in Russia, is a dictatorship of the Proletariat. And for the moment that is what it is, for that is what it must be. But that is not its aim. Its aim is a classless society. These two years of work between school and university are an experimental step in that direction. It is not that the two years in the factory shall impress the student with the hard work, miseries and unhappiness of the worker so that he will always, as engineer, physician, lawyer, have a sympathetic understanding of him and his lot, but that the future engineer, physician, lawyer may understand and have as a part of himself and be identified with the spirit, the joys, the satisfactions, the wholesomeness of the worker (such talk would be ridiculous in our country but, unbelievable as it may be, it is not ridiculous in Russia), so that he will always remain a worker whether on the bench, at the bedside or on construction. With what has already been accomplished in doing away with racial prejudices (a person being primarily a human being, quite incidentally a Jew, Turk, Armenian, Greek, Georgian or White Russian), it would be foolish to say that a doctor or an engineer by some such process, educational and social, as the Russians are working out, cannot become a worker in all that that implies for the Russian —the concept having little or nothing in common with our concept. The poor man's son in America who becomes a physician " escapes " something, " raises " himself—only to fall into the same trap at another level. The Russian boy who becomes a physician does not " escape " anything nor " raise " himself, but is privileged to join his activities with those of his father and of all other workers.

A graduate of a Russian school takes his place with his co-workers in a world of which he has some understanding, for which he is intellectually, emotionally, spiritually prepared ; he has probably been in love several times, he will before long marry (marriage will in no way interfere with his continuing to a university) and he is launched.

Q. E. D.

It occurs to me that in attempting to make this comparison I may have done nothing more, perhaps, than to paint a somewhat gloomy picture on the one hand and a somewhat idealistic picture on the other. I have read carefully what I have written. Certainly, in both instances, the picture is a composite one. It is unlikely that any one student, either American or Russian, would experience all that I have described here. In general, however, I believe that what I have written here is essentially correct.

# INDEX

For Product Safety Concerns and Information please contact our EU
representative  GPSR@taylorandfrancis.com
Taylor & Francis Verlag GmbH, Kaufingerstraße 24, 80331 München, Germany

www.ingramcontent.com/pod-product-compliance
Lightning Source LLC
Chambersburg PA
CBHW050412280326
41932CB00013BA/1829